My Life With

Ellery Queen

My Life With

Ellery Queen

A Love Story

Rose Koppel Dannay

PERFECT CRIME BOOKS

Crime@PerfectCrimeBooks.com

Perfect Crime Books™ is a registered Trademark.

Printed in the United States of America.

Library of Congress Cataloging-in-Publication Data
Dannay, Rose Koppel
My Life With Ellery Queen: A Love Story / Rose Koppel Dannay

ISBN: 978-1-935797-66-1

First Edition: February 2016

To my children and grandchildren

"...it is not too much to say that Rose Koppel Dannay, the author of this book, saved Fred's life. He had always been such a private person that after almost thirty years many of his closest Larchmont neighbors had no idea what he did for a living. Rose made it possible for him to enjoy the role of the genre's elder statesman that time and the deaths of his peers like Carr, Christie and Stout had bestowed on him."

From the Introduction by Francis M. Nevins

CONTENTS

A selection of photos begins after page 74.

Introduction: EQ 101

Francis M. Nevins

The main subject of this memoir is Frederic Dannay (1905-1982), who is much better known under the byline of Ellery Queen. Fred was the closest to a grandfather I knew and the writer who, more than anyone else, made a writer out of me. Many readers who pick up this book will already be more or less familiar with Ellery Queen. But what of those who aren't? Fred was one of the finest fiction editors of his generation. As an editor, his prime directive was: Always Keep the Reader in Mind. For those readers who need a concise survey of Ellery Queen the author and the character, I offer this introduction.

We need to begin with a glossary. Throughout these pages "Ellery" means the detective protagonist of the Ellery Queen novels and stories. "Queen" means the byline on each of Ellery's adventures in deduction and the joint pseudonym of the men who in their early twenties created both Ellery and Queen.

The first cousins who called themselves Frederic Dannay and Manfred B. Lee and called each other Manny and Danny were born in Brooklyn's Brownsville district, nine months and five blocks apart. Lee was born Manford Lepofsky on January 11, 1905; Dannay was born Daniel Nathan on October 20 of the same year. The Nathans moved upstate to Elmira when Danny was a baby and he spent his childhood in a Mark Twainish rural environment where he roamed the woods and fields and concocted elaborate schemes like charging playmates two cents apiece to see the ghost of Long John Silver. His best friend during the Elmira years was named Ellery. The Lepofskys remained in Brooklyn but Manny would visit cousin Danny in Elmira every summer and the boys would spend their time playing games of oneupmanship with each other which in altered forms they continued to play during more than forty years of collaboration. In 1917 the Nathans moved back to Brooklyn and that winter, while 12-year-old Danny was in bed with an ear infection, one of his aunts loaned him a copy of Conan Doyle's *Adventures of Sherlock Holmes*. The book so fired the boy's imagination that the next morning he got a public library card and stripped the shelves of every Holmes book he saw.

During their teens the boys became best friends. "We were cousins," Dannay said more than sixty years later, "but we were closer than brothers." One of the interests that drew and kept them together was a common passion for detective fiction, and as early as 1920, while walking or riding the streetcar to and from Boys' High, they began, Dannay said, "to experiment with ideas, to play with the strings of plot." Manny Lee went on from high school to NYU but Prohibition put an end to Meyer Nathan's liquor business and forced his son to quit Boys' High after third year and go to work. In 1926 Dannay married the first of his three wives and two years later he was working as copywriter and art director for a New York advertising agency. Lee graduated from NYU in 1926, married for the first time in 1928, and found work in the Manhattan publicity department of the Pathé movie studio. The cousins' offices were only a few blocks apart and they met for lunch almost every day.

American detective fiction in the late 1920s was dominated by the best-selling Philo Vance novels, written by art critic Willard Huntington Wright (1888-1939) under the pseudonym of S.S. Van Dine, and over their lunches Dannay and Lee discussed the idea of collaborating on a detective novel of their own in the same manner, complete with hyperintellectual sleuth and reams of erudite deduction. The announcement of a $7,500 prize contest, sponsored jointly by *McClure's Magazine* and the publisher Frederick A. Stokes, catalyzed them into serious action, and over the next several months they worked frantically on evenings, weekends and vacation time to complete a novel before the deadline. "I remember Manny Lee had to go to a wedding in Philadelphia during the time we were writing it," Fred Dannay said in 1979. "And I had to go with him, to the wedding of a complete stranger, just so we wouldn't lose the time it took to get there and back on the train." With their backgrounds in advertising and publicity they took great pains to give their protagonist a name that would be slightly unusual, easy to remember and rhythmic in sound, and after a few false starts they hit upon Ellery Queen. To comply with the contest rule that every entry be submitted under a pseudonym, the cousins made the brilliant decision to use Ellery Queen not only for their protagonist—who is himself a detective novelist, presumably under his own name—but also for their joint byline. Didn't I say we needed to begin with a glossary?

The early months of 1929 put the cousins on an emotional rollercoaster. The literary agency running the contest unofficially informed them that their submission had won, then a few days later told them that *McClure's* had gone bankrupt and its new owners had decided to award the prize to another entry. But Stokes liked their manuscript enough to make an offer for it anyway, though with a much smaller advance, and the result was the publication in August 1929 of *The Roman Hat Mystery*, under the byline of and starring Ellery Queen. In 1931, the pit of the Depression, after selling two more Queen books, Dannay and Lee gave up their day jobs and devoted full time to turning out a 90,000-word detective novel every three months for the next few years.

What was each cousin's function in the Queen partnership? Through most of their long collaboration Dannay and Lee were asked this question countless times and always replied enigmatically, drawing a veil of secrecy over their division of labor as a sort of advertising stunt to keep readers intrigued. The truth in capsule form: Dannay created the skeletons and Lee put flesh on the bones. Each Ellery Queen novel began with a plot synopsis of about 25,000 words in which Dannay would set forth the book's themes, plot, characters, clues and deductions. As soon as Lee finished absorbing that synopsis the fur would begin to fly between the cousins. After one heated argument over the phone, Lee's son Rand said, "Dad threw down a plot outline and exclaimed, 'He gives me the most ridiculous characters to work with and expects me to make them realistic!'" When the quarrels were settled, Lee would expand Dannay's synopsis into a novel of around 100,000 words and then the fighting would begin all over. "We are competitors and always have been," Dannay said. "We are always trying to out-top each other." And Lee once described a time when he and Dannay were working briefly as Hollywood screenwriters with an office directly under the studio's mimeograph department, whose duplicating machines clattered constantly. "*They* complained about the noise *we* were making!"

The cousins' first period runs from *The Roman Hat Mystery* (1929) through *The Spanish Cape Mystery* (1935) and encompasses nine novels as by and starring Ellery Queen, four more as by Barnaby Ross, and a number of short stories most of which were collected as *The Adventures of Ellery Queen* (1934)—a title deliberately echoing that first book of Sherlock Holmes tales which had so changed young Dannay's life. Although superior in plotting, characterization and style, the Queen novels of the first period were heavily influenced by the Van Dine blockbusters. The strict pattern of the titles, *The* Adjective-of-Nationality *Noun Mystery*, comes from Van Dine's pattern, *The* Six-Letter-Word *Murder Case*. Each running character in early Queen has a counterpart in Van Dine, with blockheaded Sergeant Velie for instance stemming from dumb Sergeant Heath in the Vance cases. Ellery's father, Inspector Richard Queen of the NYPD, calls on his brilliant son for help in abstruse crime puzzles much as District Attorney Markham called on that insufferable mandarin Philo Vance. Most important, it was from Van Dine that Dannay and Lee borrowed the concept of the detective as polysyllabic literatus, full of scholarly quotations, detached from people and the world, interested only in abstract problems, a Harvard-educated dilettante bibliophile who usually calls his father "pater" or "Inspector darling." Here is Ellery I as he walks on stage in *Roman Hat*: "There was a square cut to his shoulders and an agreeable swing to his body as he walked. He was dressed in oxford grey and carried a light stick. On his nose perched what seemed an incongruous note in so athletic a man—a pince-nez. But the brow above, the long delicate lines of the face, the bright eyes were those of a man of thought rather than action." In their twilight years the cousins came to hate this version of their character, whom Manny Lee derided as "the biggest prig that ever came down the pike." But those early novels are among the most richly plotted Golden Age deductive puzzles, bursting with bizarre circumstances, conflicting testimony, enigmatic clues (including that Queenian hallmark the dying message), alternative solutions, fireworks displays of virtuoso reasoning, and a constant crackle of intellectual excitement.

What makes Queen's novels stand out from the other detective fiction of the time was the cousins' insistence on playing fair. In Dannay's words, "the reader had to know everything that the detective knew, and therefore had an even chance of beating the detective before the solution was given." And they did play the game with scrupulous fairness, not only presenting all the facts (albeit quite trickily on occasion) but stopping most of the novels at a certain point to issue a formal "Challenge to the Reader" to solve the puzzle ahead of Ellery. The odds of course were stacked in favor of the house, and when Dannay once boasted to an interviewer that Queen was always "completely fair to the reader," Lee cut in: "We are fair to the reader only if he is a genius."

Among the early Queen novels perhaps the finest is *The Greek Coffin Mystery* (1932). Blind art dealer Georg Khalkis dies of heart failure in the library of his West 54th Street brownstone. Three days later the coffin is taken to the church graveyard next door and lowered into the family crypt. When the burial party returns to the house, the attorney for the estate discovers that the steel box with Khalkis's will is missing from the wall safe. The police are summoned but after two days the box is still missing. At a conference called to discuss the case are Inspector Richard Queen and a young and cocksure Ellery, who deduces that the box must be in Khalkis's coffin. An exhumation order is obtained, the coffin is opened, and inside is not the will but the decaying corpse of a second man, strangled, lying atop Khalkis's body. Inspector Queen and his men soon unearth a cornucopia of counterplots inside the Khalkis household and an assortment of intrigues outside, many rooted in the theft of a Leonardo from a British museum. After about 130 pages Ellery proposes a devilishly ingenious solution based on the amount of tea water in a percolator and the color of a dead man's tie, but he soon learns that this version of events was prepared for him to find by "the player on the other side." This is the first of four solutions to the Khalkis case, each one radiating outward from those that went before and accounting for more of the total picture. The fourth and last explanation alone embraces the entire brain-boggling web of plot and counterplot (described by Ellery as "a complex plan which requires assiduous concentration for complete comprehension") and reveals, with total fairness to the superhumanly alert reader, a stunning surprise murderer. Although not flawless, *The Greek Coffin Mystery* is probably the most involuted, brain-crushing, meticulously constructed detective novel published in the United States during the genre's golden age.

The cousins next introduced a second joint byline, Barnaby Ross, and a new detective in the person of retired Shakespearean actor Drury Lane. Driven from the stage by total deafness, Lane has recreated an Elizabethan village community on his acreage above the Hudson, populating it with down-and-out theater people who earn their keep by sporting period costumes and Shakespearean names. But this power-driven tyrant wants more: "From obeying the jerk of the master's strings, I now have the impulse to pull the strings myself, in a greater authorship than created drama." In a mad oedipal rivalry with Shakespeare's shade, Lane turns to intervening in real-world stories and in a sense rewriting them.

The Tragedy of X (1932) opens with a biographical sketch of Lane and his letter to the NYPD offering the solution to an unsolved murder case. When his deductions prove right, Inspector Thumm and District Attorney Bruno visit and thank the old man and ask his help on a problem even more bewildering. We flash back to four days earlier and eavesdrop on a cocktail party thrown by sadistic and lecherous stockbroker Harley Longstreet to celebrate his engagement to a much younger woman and make his guests squirm. Among those invited are Longstreet's browbeaten partner, his former mistress, a man who's in love with the woman he wants as his next mistress, a former lover of his present fiancée, and a corrupt politician who blames the brokers for ruinous losses in the market. After cocktails Longstreet insists that everyone go along with him to a dinner party in New Jersey. When a sudden thunderstorm makes it impossible to get a taxi for the trip to the ferry, they all board a crosstown trolley. The packed streetcar is lurching west towards the ferry slip when Longstreet reaches into his pocket and suddenly falls into the aisle, his hand pricked and bleeding in a dozen places. Once on the scene, Inspector Thumm searches the dead man's pockets and finds a cork ball riddled with needles, each one coated at both ends with pure nicotine poison. But there are too many suspects with motive and opportunity and his investigation founders. When Thumm and Bruno have recounted these facts, Drury Lane announces that he believes he knows the murderer but, due in roughly equal parts to his analysis of the situation and his lust to exercise power, refuses to say more. The next evening there's a second murder, the victim thrown from the upper deck of a ferry and crushed to pulp as the boat pulls into the Weehawken slip. Later come a spectacular murder trial, a disturbing conversation aboard a New Jersey commuter train, a third murder committed within a few feet of Lane himself, and finally, during another train ride, the unmasking.

The Tragedy of X introduced into the cousins' repertoire two motifs that were to become hallmarks. One, which they borrowed from Conan Doyle's *The Valley of Fear* (1915) and recycled throughout the novels of their first period, can't be revealed here without ruining several of those novels for those not yet familiar with them. The other, on which Dannay and Lee played variations for the rest of their careers, is the dying message clue. During a night journey on the Weehawken local which one commuter will not live to complete, Drury Lane and others involved in the case have a conversation about the last moments before death which is as central to Queen as is the locked room lecture in *The Three Coffins* (1935) to the works of John Dickson Carr. "There are no limits to which the human mind cannot soar," Lane declares, "in this unique, godlike instant before the end of life." Not only does *The Tragedy of X* offer a superb plot-puzzle and the rationale for dozens of future dying message stories, it vividly recreates a vanished time when American cities and suburbs were linked by streetcars, ferries, electric interurban lines, commuter trains—by a mass transit system that worked, and in this novel lives again.

In *The Tragedy of Y* (1932) Drury Lane visits Washington Square to probe a series of bizarre and imbecilic crimes in the doom-haunted Hatter household which for the cousins seems to be a paradigm of American society, its members rotting with greed, sadism and inertia, consenting for the sake of expected inheritances to be dehumanized in love-hate relationships with each other and with the bitch goddess of wealth and property who rules the roost. The identity of the murderer—a stunning surprise in the early Thirties but far less so today—combines with the themes of Iagoesque manipulation and despair of human nature to make this one of the darkest detective novels ever written. Lane tackled his third puzzle in *The Tragedy of Z* (1933) and died at the end of his fourth, which is aptly titled *Drury Lane's Last Case* (1933).

Ellery Queen remained active as both pseudonym and sleuth during the Drury Lane years. In *The Egyptian Cross Mystery* (1932), which may be the bloodiest pure detective novel ever, Ellery and his father spend months on the trail of a multiple murderer who beheads and crucifies victims so as to turn them into embodiments of the letter T. As usual in Golden Age whodunits with a serial killer, the crimes are not random but connected. In *The American Gun Mystery* (1933) Ellery and Inspector Queen are among the twenty thousand spectators who have piled into the New York Colosseum for the opening night of a rodeo whose main attraction is the aging silent Western film star Buck Horne, a character clearly modeled on William S. Hart. While Horne is supposed to be leading forty wild-shooting riders in a chase around the arena, someone fires a shot not in the script and the aged horseman falls to the tanbark where he's trampled to death. *The Siamese Twin Mystery* (1933) leaves Ellery and his father and the members of the household of Dr. John Xavier trapped by a forest fire in a mountaintop mansion, so that when Xavier is found shot to death in his study with a game of solitaire laid out in front of him and the torn half of the six of spades clenched between his fingers, the Queens have to tackle the crime with no outside help. The climax deftly blends nobility and lunacy: the fire reaches the house, everyone left alive holes up in the cellar, and Ellery undertakes the absurd act of exposing the murderer while they're all waiting for a horrible death. *The Chinese Orange Mystery* (1934) begins when an excruciatingly ordinary man is shown into a waiting room in the office suite of wealthy young publisher and stamp collector Donald Kirk, who happens to be a friend of Ellery's. An hour later when Kirk and Ellery enter the waiting room, it's been transformed into something out of Lewis Carroll: the rug turned upside down, pictures and clock facing the walls, floor lamps standing on their shades. Lying on the overturned rug with his brains splattered and two African spears thrust up through his pants legs and under his jacket is Mr. Nobody from Nowhere, whose every article of clothing—collar, shirt, coat, trousers, shoes—is on him backwards. The opening situation is so outré it's a shame the plot turns out neither credible nor all that complex.

Among the short stories collected in *The Adventures of Ellery Queen* (1934) "The Glass-Domed Clock" and "The Bearded Lady" are notable for complex plotting and subtle dying-message clues. In "The Mad Tea Party," Dannay's favorite short tale from this period and another proof of his fondness for Lewis Carroll, Ellery is invited to a Long Island house party that is to feature a private performance of *Alice in Wonderland,* but festive spirits are dampened when the host vanishes the morning after Ellery arrives. Then comes the delivery of a series of packages containing pairs of shoes, cabbages, chessmen and other bizarre objects. The tale indeed owes much to Carroll but Ellery's psychological war against his adversary is inspired by Poe's "Thou Art the Man."

At the tail end of Queen's first period came "The Lamp of God," one of the finest of all detective novelettes. A desperate phone call from an attorney friend takes Ellery to the raw January snowscape of Long Island. The patriarch of the maniacal Mayhew family is believed to have hidden a fortune in gold somewhere in the Poesque old mansion where he had lived and recently died, and attorney Thorne suspects that certain of the old tyrant's relatives are bent on finding and taking the treasure before it can be turned over to the old man's long-lost daughter. After a raw-nerved evening with an obese doctor, a demented old lady and an enigmatic young hired man, Ellery and the others go to bed but awaken to an event that convinces them the world has gone mad. The entire huge black house of old Sylvester Mayhew, next door to where they've been sleeping, has vanished in the night. This is one of the finest pieces of atmospheric writing in the genre, evoking chills that rise off the page into our bones. With imagery of light against darkness, sun against cold, reason against the absurd, Queen summons up the terror of a universe abandoned to the demonic, then exorcises it through the rigorous use of the instrument given us by "chance, cosmos, God, whatever you may choose to call it": the enlightening human mind.

By the mid-1930s Dannay and Lee were making excellent money not just from books but from two lucrative media which had begun to buy their work: the slick-paper magazines like *Redbook* and *Cosmopolitan* and the movies. The demands of these markets led the cousins to reconfigure their principal character into Ellery II. In second-period Queen (1936-40) the Van Dine patterned titles vanish and Ellery gradually trades in his intellectual priggishness for humanity. In Dannay's words: "We loosened the construction . . . ; we put more emphasis on character development and background; we put more emphasis on human-interest situations. . . . We turned to commercialism because we frankly wanted to make more money." Compared with the classics of period one, much of the cousins' output of the late 1930s suffers from thin plots, overdoses of tedious boy-meets-girl byplay, and characters tailored to please story editors at the slick magazine suites and the studios. But in the longer view the exploits of Ellery II served at least in part to open up the deductive puzzle and make room within its cerebral rigor for more of the virtues of mainstream storytelling. In several short tales and in the novels *The Devil to Pay* and *The Four of Hearts* (both 1938) Ellery works as a Hollywood screenwriter, paralleling the cousins' brief stints at Columbia, Paramount and MGM. Hoping to make their character more appealing to the mass media, Dannay and Lee had Ellery become involved with lovely gossip columnist Paula Paris, a prose amalgam of the heroines from Hollywood's screwball comedies of the time. And perhaps screwball is the best one-word description of Queen's take on movieland. "The place was filled with crazy people," Dannay said in 1979. "I told Manny even if I had to dig ditches for the rest of my life, I wasn't coming back." *The New Adventures of Ellery Queen* (1940), which brought together all the short cases of Ellery II plus "The Lamp of God" and a few others from the early years, concluded this phase of the saga.

By 1940 Fred and Mary Dannay and their sons were living the suburban life in Great Neck, Long Island and Fred was close to reaching his goal as a book collector: owning a copy of every volume of detective-crime short stories ever published. Manny Lee, divorced from his first wife, was sharing a Park Avenue apartment with his daughters. The cousins put in 12-hour workdays at their respective homes and met once a week at a rented office to consolidate their material. Both men were chain smokers and their workplace atmosphere tended to be on the thick side. On the office floor they kept a tattered brown envelope labeled IDEAS.

And at that time they needed every idea they could conjure up. Since June of 1939, when *The Adventures of Ellery Queen* series had debuted on the CBS radio network, they had had to turn out a 60-minute script every week. Among the most complex of the early audio adventures is "The Last Man Club" (June 25, 1939), in which Ellery (Hugh Marlowe) and his secretary and love interest Nikki Porter (Marian Shockley), a new character created by the cousins to attract female listeners, witness a hit-and-run and are propelled by the victim's dying words into the affairs of a survivor-take-all group to which the dead man belonged—the first but far from the last death-plagued tontine in the Queen canon. Some of the best Queen radio plays were collected in *The Adventure of the Murdered Moths* (2005).

Radio work gave Dannay and Lee a steady income but left them no time for any other writing. In September 1940 the show left the air, and the next fifteen months were among the most fruitful in the cousins' lives. Dannay, the historian and bibliophile of the duo, used his library of detective-crime short story collections as the basis for editing *101 Years' Entertainment* (1941), the definitive anthology of short mystery fiction between Poe and Pearl Harbor. When he found countless first-rate tales for which that mammoth volume had no room, he persuaded publisher Lawrence E. Spivak to launch *Ellery Queen's Mystery Magazine (EQMM)*, the genre's premier periodical, which Dannay actively edited from its first issue (Fall 1941) until shortly before his death more than forty years later. It was also during these fifteen months that the cousins commenced their third and richest period as writers. Ellery III is no longer a detached Philo Vance clone but a human being scarred by the horrors he encounters, and the Queen novels are no longer problems in deduction but much closer to mainstream fiction.

Calamity Town (1942) opens on the afternoon of August 6, 1940, when Ellery steps off the train and into Wrightsville, a small tight-knit vividly portrayed community that with the outbreak of war in Europe has become a boomtown. He needs a place to stay while writing his next novel but no hotel rooms or furnished houses are available except for one which has developed a reputation as a jinx. John F. and Hermione Wright had built a house next to their own as a wedding present for their daughter Nora and her fiancé Jim Haight, but Jim had disappeared the day before the wedding and later a prospective purchaser had died of a heart attack in the house. Ellery rents the place and quickly bonds with the entire Wright family, especially with youngest daughter Pat, whose steady is the county prosecutor. Then Jim Haight returns to town, reconciles with and marries Nora. The newlyweds move into the house built for them three years before and day by day over months the marriage goes sour and the atmosphere thickens with hints that Jim is planning to kill his wife. At the Wrights' New Year's Eve party one of the drinks raised to toast the beginning of 1941 turns out to be poisoned, and Wrightsville's first homicide in years tears apart both the family and the town. The investigation, public reactions, a sensational trial and what happens afterward are not just pieces of a puzzle (though a neat plot is hidden among them) but nightmares happening to people one cares about, with Ellery no longer the controlling mind but a man in a muddle, powerless to affect events and contributing nothing until the final chapter.

Calamity Town, Dannay said, was "the best book that we thought we had written up to that time." But no national magazine made the offer for serialization rights that the cousins had expected and no editor could explain why not. "We'd better find another basket for our eggs," Dannay told Lee. "If you can be turned down with no reason apparent on the best book you've ever written....then you've got to do something else." The obvious contender for "something else" was radio, and the cousins' agent soon found a new network and sponsor for the continuing audio exploits of Ellery Queen. In January 1942 the series returned to the air and Dannay and Lee to the old grind of a script a week, although several of the "new" adventures were tighter rewrites of 60-minute dramas from the program's first months. Manny Lee happened to visit the NBC studio during a rehearsal on April 1 and met actress Kaye Brinker, who was featured in the week's story. They began dating at once, were married on July 4, and stayed together until Lee's death almost 29 years later. Except for summer rerun cycles and several hiatus periods the series was heard weekly on one network or another until the spring of 1948. "A new plot every week knocked me out," Dannay said. Even after mid-1945 when his function of providing a weekly plot outline was taken over by others, notably Anthony Boucher, the demands of *EQMM* left him little time for Ellery Queen novels.

The cousins had taken such care and pains over the creation of Wrightsville that it's no wonder they had Ellery go back in *The Murderer Is a Fox* (1945). In the summer of 1944 a nerve-shattered war hero returns home after receiving some anonymous letters intimating that his wife was unfaithful during his service as a fighter pilot in Asia. Twelve years earlier Captain Davy Fox's mother had been murdered and his father sentenced to life imprisonment for the crime, and the boy's adolescence had been a nightmare of failed attempts to escape the stigma and the fear of his own "tainted blood." As Davy wrestles with a growing compulsion to kill his wife, she goes for help to Ellery, who concludes that the only way to release Davy from the trap in which the past holds him is to reopen the old case and try to prove that his father did not kill his mother. Ellery's meticulous reconstruction of exactly what happened in the house of Bayard and Jessica Fox on June 14, 1932 is carried out with the intellectual tools of the historian and generates the sort of excitement that every conscientious historian feels while on the hunt for the truth of the past. Like many Queen novels to come, this one ends with a false or partial solution followed by a second solution that is both final and shattering.

"In the beginning it was without form, a darkness that kept shifting like dancers." With that echo from Genesis I:2 we return yet again to Wrightsville in *Ten Days' Wonder* (1948). Howard Van Horn, sculptor son of a multimillionaire, comes in desperation to Ellery after a series of amnesic blackouts that began on the night of his father Diedrich's marriage to the beautiful Sally whom Diedrich had raised from childhood. Psychiatrists have failed to free Howard from his obsessive fear that he has done or will do something horrible during a blackout. Ellery agrees to stay at the Van Horn mansion in Wrightsville and watch over this tormented young man but before long he finds himself drawn into the hopeless trap in which Howard and Sally are caught. He reluctantly agrees to act as their go-between with an anonymous blackmailer and comes close to being jailed for grand theft. A missing necklace, a midnight chase through a storm-tossed graveyard and a night-prowling religious fanatic combine with less theatrical elements to sustain the sense of menace among a cast of (excluding Ellery himself) only four central characters. In the final quarter of the novel there is a murder, followed by Ellery's virtuoso reconstruction of the crime, capped by an even more thunderous solution, revealed by Ellery to no one but the murderer, who will remind some of Drury Lane, others of Iago, and a great many of the biblical God. Beneath the mind-boggling plot which Dannay spent years working out, *Ten Days' Wonder* is an audacious, ambitious attempt to recreate the cosmic drama of Western culture since the Enlightenment: the penetration through the facade of infinite knowledge and love to the sadistic beast beneath, the demand of reason and decency for God's death.

At the start of the next and perhaps finest Queen novel, *Cat of Many Tails* (1949), Ellery has renounced his habit of intervening in others' lives. "Just let me be....I've given all that up. I'm not interested any longer." Racked with guilt over his responsibility for others' deaths and perhaps over his deicide victory in the Van Horn tragedy, he has detached himself. It's a scorching Manhattan summer a few years after the end of World War II, and the reminders of Hiroshima, the Nazi death camps, the Cold war, the division of Vienna, the first Arab-Israeli conflict, the anti-Communist witch hunts and the threat of nuclear annihilation generate an atmosphere thick with impending holocaust. But the world and national news headlines are dwarfed by local headlines that convey the same message of mortality. A serial killer is loose in the city. Six people strangled in less than three months, each victim totally different from fellow victims in ethnic roots, economic worth, social position, neighborhood of residence and every other way. The faceless bachelor from the Gramercy Park district, the aging prostitute living above Times Square, the struggling shoe salesman from Chelsea, the madcap heiress who loved the subways, the bitter paralytic of East 102nd Street, the black girl from Harlem and the later victims of the Cat share only the cord of Indian tussah silk knotted about each one's neck. The bait of involvement is dangled before Ellery again with all its pain and risk and once again he snaps at it, immersing himself in the Cat hunt until like his father and the police commissioner and the mayor and everyone else he's ready to drop in his tracks from the exhaustion and frustration of strategy conferences, press releases, radio addresses, coordination among agencies, liaison with psychiatrists, confrontations with neighborhood self-defense committees, endless reviewing of files and plodding up blind alleys until, suddenly and beyond human expectation, the obvious yet subtle link connecting all the victims and making sense of the carnage leaps into sight. Once again the apparent solution is topped by another and once again Ellery is left shattered.

In key scenes at the beginning, middle and end of this powerful novel, Ellery receives instruction from a father figure: first from Inspector Queen who spurs him to involve himself again, then in a dream from the titan Prometheus who in Greek mythology was the father of civilization, finally from the Viennese psychiatrist Dr. Seligmann, the "grandfather of the tribe," who has seen all the terrors in the world and the human heart. "I do not read newspapers since the war begins. I, I do not like to suffer....For me there is today this room, tomorrow cremation, unless the authorities cannot agree to allow it, in which case they may stuff me and place me in the clock tower of the *Rathaus* and I shall keep reminding them of the time." Queen in *Cat of Many Tails* shows a fastidious contempt for humanity in the abstract but infuses life into countless individual people including the Cat's victims, who are never seen alive but are resurrected, as it were, in the words of others. From the interweaving of victims and survivors and bystanders and investigators, from the vivid pictures of where and how each one lives and what he or she thinks and hopes and fears, there emerges a portrait of the city as a living character itself. Queen encompasses countless aspects of urban life from the racial turmoil to the struggle against the heat, from the chaos of a full-scale riot to the simple delights of radio programs like *The Shadow* and *Stella Dallas*. It's the most abundant book in the canon, offering permanent testimony to the potential of mystery fiction.

No Queen novel of the 1950s quite equals these two masterpieces but many are worth exploring. In *The Origin of Evil* (1951) Ellery returns to Hollywood, no longer the goofy madhouse of the Thirties but a grim place whose movie industry is under siege from television. His attempt to finish a novel is frustrated when 19-year-old Laurel Hill knocks on his door with the claim that her wealthy foster father was literally frightened to death two weeks earlier upon finding a dead dog on his doorstep. Roger Priam, the dead man's partner in the jewelry business, has also been sent some strange objects, and Priam's lush exotic wife quickly entangles Ellery in a household that includes an enigmatic secretary, a wandering philatelist and a young man who lives in a treehouse. As Ellery probes more deeply into the Hill and Priam households, the bizarre objects—a mess of dead frogs, an empty wallet, a portfolio of worthless stock certificates—keep popping up. Eventually he discerns the pattern and his solution, followed as usual by a second even more breathtaking, ties plot and theme into an organic whole. The leitmotif of the book is Darwinian biology and the answer to the implied question in its title is Humankind. "People mean trouble....There's too much trouble in this world."

As an editor Dannay had long believed that a mystery anthology should be held together by a central concept or theme, and he and Lee extended this tenet to their third collection of Ellery Queen short stories. Each of the twelve tales in *Calendar of Crime* (1952) had begun life as a script for the Queen radio series which Manny Lee later rewrote in prose form for publication in *EQMM,* and each adventure centers on an event associated with a particular month of the year, from New Year's Day through Washington's Birthday and Memorial Day and Hallowe'en to (of course) Thanksgiving and Christmas. The finest of the dozen are "The Inner Circle," in which Ellery investigates the deaths of several members of a survivor-take-all tontine among the 1913 graduating class of Eastern University, and "The Dauphin's Doll," an impossible-crime puzzle with Ellery trying to protect a 49-carat diamond crown from a master thief who's boasted that he'll steal it while it's on display at a department store on the day before Christmas.

Those tales, stemming as they do from radio plays of the middle Forties, are rather light and amusing in tone. That the Queen novels from the late Forties and early Fifties are so much darker stems largely from events in the life of Fred Dannay. His first wife had died of cancer in 1945. Two years later he married again and bought a colonial house in Larchmont, a suburb forty minutes by train from Manhattan, and in 1948 Hilda Dannay gave birth to their first and only child. "[Stephen] was born prematurely at seven months and weighing less than two pounds. He was the miracle baby of Doctors Hospital in New York City. We didn't realize for about a year that he—that the boy had had brain damage at birth...so severe that the child, who had an absolutely angelic face, never walked and never talked....I was aware long before my wife that one of these days the tragedy would be capped by the death of that child. Actually he lived till he was six years old." It is to the short unhappy life of Stephen Dannay that we owe the pervasive birth-death themes in several Queen novels beginning with *Cat of Many Tails*, which grew out of an anecdote told to Fred by one of the infant's doctors over dinner in the hospital cafeteria. And in a sense it's Stephen who inspired the only novel Dannay wrote without a collaborator.

The Golden Summer (1953), published under his birth name Daniel Nathan, was written as a kind of therapy against his son's impending death, a nostalgic reenactment of his own vanished childhood and an exorcism of his anguished middle life. The scene is Elmira in the summer of 1915 and the storyline deals with the business adventures of 10-year-old Danny Nathan, a skinny bespectacled physical weakling who's shrewd and nimble-witted enough to talk himself out of any spot and to manipulate his playmates out of their loose change. He displays the ghost of Long John Silver for a two-cent admission fee, raffles off a damaged copy of the latest Sherlock Holmes novel, and even adds a dime to his hoard through a splendiferous one-upmanship contest with his city cousin "Telford." *The Golden Summer* is at root a book-length *double entendre*: the season of innocent security and peace, the season when Danny tricked his contemporaries out of $4.73. Fred's brutally honest self-portrait provides the key to countless features of the Ellery Queen world, including the image of Ellery I as the weak-eyed young genius who dominates his environment by the force of his mind and perhaps the Iagoesque quality of so many of the murderers exposed by Ellery in all his incarnations.

The Glass Village (1954) is doubly unusual: one of only two Queen novels without Ellery and the other familiar series characters, and the only Queen book set in the midst of the cultural terror that marked the years of Joe McCarthy and HUAC and the blacklist. In the withered New England hamlet of Shinn Corners live exactly 36 people, most of them embittered puritanical bigots. Judge Lewis Shinn is spending a week at his vacation home in the village where he was born, bonding with his nephew Johnny, a war veteran who had witnessed Hiroshima and was sexually mutilated in Korea and calls himself "a vegetable" and "the missing link between the flora and the fauna." What precipitates Johnny's slow journey back to the human race is the bludgeoning to death of 91-year-old artist Fanny Adams in her studio one rainy afternoon. A foreign-looking tramp who had passed through the village shortly before the murder is instantly tagged as the perpetrator, hunted down, beaten and almost lynched by the outraged citizens of Shinn Corners, who refuse to turn over their prey to the state police and insist on trying him themselves. To avert a gun battle Judge Shinn agrees to preside at that trial, a proceeding aswarm with legal gaffes, designed to placate the townspeople for now and be reversed by an appellate court later. Among the jurors is Johnny Shinn. Ten of the other jurors admit under oath that they're already certain the tramp is guilty. The bailiff, the court reporter, most of the jurors and even the judge testify for the prosecution. Judge Shinn takes over as prosecutor while the prosecutor testifies against the defendant. Defense counsel fails to object to gross violations of his client's rights but fights loudly over the admissibility of trivia. The judge bangs the darning egg he's using as a gavel and hands down legal rulings he knows are dead wrong. This study in due process on the other side of the rabbit hole is also one of the finest Queen novels of the Fifties, replete with bizarre clues and inspired misdirection and even a sort of dying message, and with dark overtones like Johnny's reflection that "man was a chaos without rhyme or reason; that he blundered about like a maddened animal in the delicate balance of the world, smashing and disrupting, eager only for his own destruction."

In *Q.B.I.: Queen's Bureau of Investigation* (1955) the cousins brought together most of the Ellery Queen short-short stories (several based on scripts from the Queen radio series) which had been published regularly in *This Week* since 1949 and reprinted just as regularly in *EQMM*. "Among the best tales in the collection are "My Queer Dean!," in which an academic's linguistic spoonerisms help Ellery solve the theft of $10,000 from a university administration building, and "Snowball in July," where an entire train apparently vanishes one summer morning on a straight stretch of track between two upstate New York whistlestops six minutes apart.

Queen's third period ended with *The Finishing Stroke* (1958), in which the cousins nostalgically recreated Ellery's young manhood and their own. It's December 1929, shortly after publication of the author-detective's first novel (titled, of course, *The Roman Hat Mystery*), and Ellery is one of the guests invited to a 12-day house party at the estate of his publisher's former partner. The holiday mood begins to dissolve when a costumed Santa distributes gifts and then vanishes. Next some bizarre objects start popping up—a sandalwood ox, a toy house, a tiny lead camel—each accompanied by a piece of doggerel derived from "The Twelve Days of Christmas." Then an unidentified body is discovered in the library, more weird gifts turn up, blackmail and a love quadrangle and a second murder enter the picture, and young Ellery can shed no light until chance again throws the case in his path 28 years later. The characters in *The Finishing Stroke* are little more than line drawings, the prose is simple and unadorned, the plot elements deadeningly overfamiliar—the snowbound house-party, the thirteenth guest, murder with an antique dagger in the lordly mansion's library, a séance, identical twins, mysterious clues dropped by an unseen hand— and the signals are clear all through this reduction of the mystery genre to its bare fundamentals that after completing their elegy to "the lovely past" Dannay and Lee would write no more.

And for the next several years they didn't. Manny Lee, who had moved his family to a 63-acre farm in Roxbury, Connecticut, became active in civic affairs, served a term as Justice of the Peace and beat his playwright neighbor Arthur Miller in an election for a seat on the library board. Fred Dannay sold his huge collection of detective story volumes to the University of Texas and spent two semesters on campus as a professor of creative writing.

If Dannay wanted to work on more Ellery Queen books he was stymied by the fact that Lee was suffering from a prolonged case of writer's block and could no longer do his share of the collaborations. In 1960 the cousins' literary agent came up with a scheme to expand Queen's readership beyond the slowly fading genre of pure detective fiction and into the booming field of original softcover crime novels without detection. Contingent on Dannay's and Lee's approval, the Scott Meredith literary agency arranged for a cycle of non-series paperback suspensers, to be ghost-written by other Meredith clients for a flat fee of around $2,000 per book and published as by Ellery Queen, with royalties to be split by Dannay and Lee after the agency took its commission. Lee, who had eight children to support and was still plagued by writer's block, favored the proposal. Dannay was violently against it but felt that his cousin's financial and creative problems left him little choice but to go along. The manuscripts written by the various ghosts were submitted to Manny, who edited and sometimes heavily revised them as Fred edited and sometimes heavily revised the stories he bought for *EQMM*. But Dannay refused to read any of the books published under this scheme and terminated the arrangement soon after his cousin's death.

Five years after publication of *The Finishing Stroke*, the Meredith agency signed other writers, with no credits in the mystery field but high reputations in science fiction, to assume Lee's function and turn Dannay's complex synopses into new hardcover exploits of Ellery Queen. The Queen novels of this fourth and final period are marked by a zest for experiment within the strict deductive tradition and by a retreat from all semblance of plausibility into what Dannay liked to call "fun and games," i.e. a potpourri of stylized plots and characters and dozens of motifs lifted from earlier Queen material.

First and finest of the fourth-period novels was *The Player on the Other Side* (1963), written by Theodore Sturgeon from Dannay's lengthy outline. The setting is York Square, in Manhattan but surely not of it, an isolated pocket of the past at each corner of which stands a castle inhabited by one of four cousins, with a diamond-shaped park in the square's center. The unifying image of course is chess: York Square is the board, each dwelling in the position of a rook, or castle, at the start of a game. The cousins are required to live in these castles by the terms of Nathaniel York Senior's will, which leaves them his millions in equal shares after ten years of residence, with the share of any cousin who dies during the decade to be split among the survivors—our old friend the tontine redux. This time however we know the murderer from the outset. The person who's sending a paper polygon stamped with a cryptic initial to each York in turn before killing them is Walt, the weak-brained and zombie-like handyman who serves a caretaker for all four cousins. But Walt is a simple soldier following orders, carrying out the detailed written instructions of someone signing himself Y, who is using Walt the way Iago used Othello, as a living murder weapon. In *Cat of Many Tails* Inspector Queen had prodded Ellery out of guilt-haunted detachment by dangling the bait of involvement with the real world, but in *Player* he goads his son out of the real world onto the chessboard of York Square. As the murders continue, as Ellery several times comes achingly close to the part of the truth we have known from the beginning, as possibilities multiply and secrets are bared, the pattern of the web slowly becomes clearer until at last Ellery encounters the player on the other side—who is revealed to be not just a human being but symbolically the primal Y, YHWH, God. Whose death, as in *Ten Days' Wonder*, is witnessed by Ellery at the climax.

The next Queen novel, probably the most controversial book in the canon, was written from Dannay's outline by Avram Davidson. *And On the Eighth Day* (1964) is set in the war-ravaged spring of 1944. Ellery gets lost driving across the Western desert, chances upon a religious-socialist community in the wilderness, and soon discovers that his coming had been foretold by the community's sacred book. All property in the valley of Quenan is held in common, no act of violence has been committed for generations, the word war is not in the lexicon, no one is alienated from the work he or she performs, the earth and humankind are in natural harmony—clearly this is Eden before the fall. Ellery's coming marks the beginning of a time of troubles foretold in the sacred book, and on the third night of his visit there is a murder. The plot doesn't and under the circumstances can't be expected to generate much intellectual excitement, but Queen structures his religious and historical analogies so as to create a sense of "the recurrence of the great and the famous across the shifting planes of space-time" and to generate an intuition of the presence of something that the human mind can never fathom. "It is too much....it's more than reason can bear. Too much, an infinite complexity beyond the grasp of man. Acknowledge. Acknowledge and depart."

After a few more books with Avram Davidson performing the Manny Lee function, Lee overcame his writer's block and collaborated with Dannay on such late Ellery Queen novels as the excellent *Face to Face* (1967) and the well-meaning but awkward *The Last Woman in His Life* (1970). Most of Ellery's as yet uncollected short cases were assembled in *Q.E.D.: Queen's Experiments in Detection* (1968). The book's last and finest tale is "Abraham Lincoln's Clue," which brings together bibliomania, philately, history and the art of the riddle as Ellery tries to locate a lost first printing of Poe's "The Purloined Letter" autographed by both the author and our sixteenth president.

In the late 1960s Manny Lee suffered several heart attacks and, on doctor's orders, lost a great deal of weight. It didn't save him. On April 2, 1971, the 65-year-old Lee had another attack and died on the way to the Waterbury hospital. He never saw a copy of the last Ellery Queen novel. In *A Fine and Private Place* (1971) Ellery investigates a series of bizarre crimes in the household of the squat and bestial tycoon Nino Importuna, who was born on September 9, 1899 and lives in a 9-story building at 99 East 99ᵗʰ Street and in countless ways is obsessed with the number 9. The orgy of variations on this theme—including links between the conception and development of the murderer's Byzantine scheme and the conception and development of a baby—is almost enough to make one overlook the unlikeliness of the plot.

At first Fred planned to continue the series, either alone or with a new partner, but in 1972 his second wife died of cancer like his first 27 years before, and with her death he began dying by inches. The only thing that kept him functioning was the inexorable work schedule that *EQMM* and the anthologies he continued to edit demanded of him. He abandoned all thought of writing more Ellery Queen novels, saying it would be disloyal to Manny's memory. Photographs of him taken in 1973 show the empty, devastated face of a man waiting for the dark to claim him.

In November 1975 he married for the third time, and it is not too much to say that Rose Koppel Dannay, the author of this book, saved Fred's life. He had always been such a private person that after almost thirty years many of his closest Larchmont neighbors had no idea what he did for a living. Rose made it possible for him to enjoy the role of the genre's elder statesman that time and the deaths of his peers like Carr, Christie and Stout had bestowed on him.

In his eighth decade Dannay received more media exposure than in all his previous life. First came the 60-minute TV series (NBC, 1975-76) starring Jim Hutton and David Wayne as Ellery and Inspector Queen. This was followed by guest lectures at the University of California, two appearances on the Dick Cavett show, superstar treatment at the 1978 International Crime Writers Congress, interviews with *Playboy* and *People* and countless other periodicals, a testimonial dinner celebrating the 50ᵗʰ anniversary of *The Roman Hat Mystery*, an invitation to Tokyo for the premiere of a Japanese movie based on *Calamity Town*—it was a miracle he got any work done at all. But after he turned 75 failing health forced him to curtail more and more activities. He was hospitalized three times and, over the Labor Day weekend of 1982, his heart stopped.

His death meant more than the end of a great tradition in

detective fiction. Both separately and together, Frederic Dannay and Manfred B. Lee contributed so abundantly to so many different aspects of the genre—novels, novelettes, short stories, radio dramas, anthologies, magazines, bibliographic and scholarly studies—that Anthony Boucher, the founding father of intelligent and informed commentary on the field, needed just one short sentence to sum up their accomplishments: "Ellery Queen *is* the American detective story."

Francis M. Nevins, who has twice won an Edgar from the Mystery Writers of America for his scholarly work, is the author of *Ellery Queen: The Art of Detection* (2013) and *Judges & Justice & Lawyers & Law: Exploring the Legal Dimensions of Fiction and Film* (2014). He is the editor of *Love and Night: Unknown Stories by Cornell Woolrich* (2007) and many other Woolrich studies. More than a score of his own short fictions have been assembled with author's notes in *Night Forms* (2012).

My Life With

Ellery Queen

In the Beginning...
New Year's Eve, 1974

New Year's Eve, 1974. Larchmont, New York.

There must have been something about the tilt of his head as he listened to someone speaking. The upward gesture of his hand was as though he were indicating "Wait, that's not how it is," and made me feel he had something important to say.

I had come into the living room rather quietly. I didn't want to disturb the flow of conversation between the people I knew, whose faces I could see, and this other person with his back to the door, the slightly round-shouldered, broad-backed man in a dark suit.

This, I assumed, was my dinner partner, the odd-man-out whom I, the odd-woman-out, was being set up with for a New Year's Eve party at my best friend's home.

I knew only a few things about him, all rather unfavorable. My friend had said, "He's really too old for you, and he's not a well man." Worse, she told me, "From what I've heard, he has no sense of humor."

Why in the world had I accepted this invitation?

Of course I knew why. I didn't want to be alone. I had been widowed the previous April after a wonderful 34-year marriage. I was just beginning to come out of my feelings of loneliness and despair. And unattached men "of a certain age" available on New Year's Eve were hard, if not impossible, to find.

Fred always called that night one of the luckiest of his life. I felt that way too.

I'll never forget the expression on Fred's face as I came toward him for our formal introduction. Suddenly he was a straight-backed man, standing tall, with a look of surprise and, it seemed, pleasure on his face.

"Where did you come from?" he asked me. "I didn't hear the door open."

It wasn't until I knew him better, until I found out who Fred Dannay really was, that I realized the significance of his remark. He was always paying attention to clues, to the unexpected, the element of surprise, life's little and big mysteries that needed to be solved. He was Ellery Queen, the famous mystery writer. But I didn't know it then, and wouldn't until much later.

I had come directly from my office in New York City and had been upstairs changing into my party clothes, a beige ultra suede gown, so of course no door bell had rung, nor had a door opened and closed. How mysterious...

I smiled broadly and replied: "I came from heaven, of course."

From the expression on Fred's face, he looked as though he believed it. Later he would tell me that I had looked like an angel to him. He also confessed that his heart was beating so fast he had to sit down.

After our introduction, I left him to greet other friends. I felt Fred's eyes on me as I walked around the room. After a few pleasantries with the others, I returned with a drink in my hand to sit beside him.

He was very quiet, almost speechless it seemed. One of us had to start the conversation, so I started to tell Fred about myself, my work, my art, my family. He asked many questions. That was his style of conversation. I didn't know whether it was his way of staying in the background and protecting his privacy or whether he was just uneasy in a social situation.

He appeared so tense I tried to make him feel comfortable. As I answered his questions as openly as seemed appropriate, he seemed to relax. But I had to keep myself from feeling as though he was the professor and I the student trying to pass an oral exam. Had I given the right answers?

It was time for dinner, and our hostess was about to seat us. "I hope we're not separated," he told me. Needless to say, we weren't, and when he realized this, he was naïve enough to be surprised and pleased. Or at least he pretended to be.

Over dinner he seemed to open up. He talked about himself, and a reservoir of troubles and sadness came pouring out. It was so intense I almost felt engulfed by it. He seemed unaware of the other guests. It was as if he and I were the only two people at that table. I was embarrassed that I was unable to participate in the general conversation, but Fred was unyielding in his attempts to hold my attention. I suddenly realized how much he needed to have someone listen to what he had lived through over the years. So I sat quietly and listened.

His first wife, Mary, had died of cancer in 1945 and left him a widower with two young sons. Two years later he had married Hilda. A year later she gave birth to a premature baby who had been born with brain damage and had to be institutionalized. He died at age 6. Fred talked to me about the last years of Hilda's life as she fought lung cancer. After she died in 1972, he told me, he started dating a woman he had known for years. The relationship became serious, and they had planned on getting married, but it never happened. She was diagnosed with terminal stomach cancer and died.

I was very sympathetic and tried to say the right things while thinking: What a sad unlucky man this was. No wonder he didn't have a sense of humor. No wonder he couldn't summon up any laughter.

Caught up in his web of sadness, I started to feel sorry for myself. I had my own share of sadness, and I needed some cheerfulness. It was New Year's Eve. I wanted it to be a time of optimism.

I tried to turn Fred's attention to our beautifully prepared and tasty dinner. That didn't work. He explained that he was a diabetic and had already eaten at his required time at home. This meal was an extra snack for him. For me, it was a well-deserved feast. When the dessert arrived, a Black Forest cake with whipped cream, I was astonished that this diabetic dived right into it. "I do cheat on my diet occasionally," he confessed. "And I just can't resist chocolate."

"Then won't it be nice if the New Year turns out to be as sweet as this cake you shouldn't be eating?" I replied.

For the first time that evening, he smiled.

After dinner we all went into the living room to await our champagne to toast the New Year. Fred would let no one separate us and stood firmly at my side. By this time, though, he seemed more relaxed and even started to take part in the general conversation. But I noticed that he never really laughed, as the rest of us did, at someone's amusing story. Oh, he smiled, but, I thought, what a repressed man this is. Somehow that made me even more determined to make him feel that life could be worthwhile.

At midnight, as we all raised our glasses, all of us kissed each other warmly. I turned to Fred, who was quietly standing beside me, and said, "Watch it, Fred. You're about to be kissed by a perfect stranger, and I really do mean perfect." I knew I had startled him, but I kissed him anyway. I knew he was pleased.

"Thank you," he said. "That was beautiful."

I was pleased with myself for having the courage to be so bold, and I was pleased with his reaction. I knew he would never have taken the initiative.

Somewhere around 2 a.m., everyone started to leave. As Fred and I said good-night, he clung to my hand and rather shyly said, "I hope you're staying overnight. If you are, may I call you tomorrow?"

"Yes," I said, "I'm staying overnight. And yes, you may call me. As long as it's not before 11 a.m."

He held my hand even tighter and told me, "I'll try to wait, but just know I'll be up early, thinking of what to say to you." Was that my heart skipping a beat?

The next morning, right at 11 a.m., the phone rang. Yes, it was Fred.

"I think I have the right words," I heard him say. "It was a sheer delight to meet you." I was flattered. "May I pick you up so that we might spend some time together this afternoon?"

"Yes," I replied. "It will be nice to see you again." I was trying to be as polite and formal as he seemed to be.

At 2 p.m. sharp, Fred arrived in an old and stodgy gray four-door Pontiac. It was a lovely afternoon. The sun was shining, the air clear and frosty, as Fred drove slowly through Larchmont. And then he popped the question. "Would you like to see my home?"

Oh-oh, I thought. Will this mild-mannered man attack me in the confines of his bachelor's quarters? I was so new to this. Nevertheless I said, "Thank you. That would be nice."

We drove up a winding road with neatly planted shrubs and manicured lawns but not a sidewalk in sight. To a New Yorker, this was the country. The houses, on three-quarter acre lots, were all English Tudor and American Colonial, all painted white with the only visible differences being the colors of the trim, shutters, and front doors. Fred's were a deep blue. The grounds were beautiful, but inside it felt dark and lifeless. The curtains were drawn and the walls, painted or papered, were done in a nondescript shade of green, the wall-to-wall carpeting in a darker but equally nondescript green.

Fred took me on a tour of the first floor. There was a huge breakfront in the living room, filled with books that could be seen through the leaded glass doors. Later I would learn that these were rare books, all first editions and one of the finest collections of English poetry. They were Fred's pride and joy.

There was a beautiful fireplace that had been painted white and above it a striking oil painting, a portrait of Fred.

At the far end of the room was a grand piano of polished ebony which added its own glow to the room, at least from the few exposed areas. The top was covered with family photographs, bric-a-brac, and more books. Even the piano bench was a depository for books that rose well above the keyboard in precarious piles. Fred had taken piano lessons, and even tried composing, but he had decided that it was taking his time and mind away from his writing, and writing was his priority.

There were books piled high on both sides of every chair in the room. My eye caught the stunning collection of antique fairy lamps, tiny glass oil lamps reflecting their myriad colors in the light of the large bay window at the front of the room.

There were more in the complementary bay window in the formal dining room, which housed not only a large rock maple table with two matching armchairs and two side chairs, but also a sideboard, a corner curio cabinet, a Winthrop secretary, a lovely vitrine, and more dining chairs along the wall, unmatched, but each an interesting antique in itself. What dominated the room, however, was a huge television, Fred's dining companion.

The other room that Fred showed me, with apologies for its

cluttered state, was his study. It was a small room with a massive desk covered with piles of papers. Floor-to-ceiling bookcases were filled not only with books but with more papers. In the corner was an old red leather chair, its springs broken under the load of more books and papers.

Clutter and the smell of cigars and a specially mixed pipe tobacco aside, Fred's house was surprisingly clean. Later I would learn that a faithful housekeeper was responsible. Hattie had been coming on a daily basis for the previous two decades. She cleaned, cooked, washed, ironed, and sent Fred's suits to the cleaners. She would continue for ten more years, until Fred's death.

Throughout the tour I was conscious only of being alone with a man I hardly knew. Fred seemed nervous too.

"Would you like a drink?" he asked when the tour was over.

I hesitated to answer, thinking it was too early for wine or cocktails.

"I can make us some tea very easily," he told me. "And I have cookies for us too."

So much for a sophisticated Hollywood-style afternoon rendezvous! Was I relieved, or disappointed?

We had our tea in the dining room, and from the look on Fred's face I sensed he was preparing to tell me more of his troubles. I didn't think I could stand any more of it and I didn't want to jabber away about myself as I had done the night before. I said, quite firmly, "Today, Fred, I want you to tell me about your work, your family and your children."

His response:

"About my work, I edit short stories for a magazine. About my children, I'm not very close to them. My older son is a school teacher and lives in Long Island and calls me about once a week or every other week; my younger son is a lawyer and lives in New York City. I speak to him more frequently because he handles my legal affairs. My only other living relative is my sister, who lives in Philadelphia. We rarely call each other."

Every indication was that, outside of a few dinner invitations to friends' homes, his whole life revolved around his work and his television, which he admitted was an addiction. He even confessed to watching a soap opera every afternoon. He didn't go to the theater, concerts, or even movies.

"You know," he confided, "there are days when I don't speak to a soul, particularly if my office doesn't have any reason to call me. Some days I'll go to the supermarket, not because I need anything. I just want to be in the physical presence of people."

Fred continued:

"One evening, after an especially lonely day, I rang the doorbell of my neighbor across the street. I was so embarrassed but so desperate. I asked if I might visit with them for a short time. They must have been tired from their own day's activities and weren't too receptive or aware of my acute need. Soon after I arrived, they suggested, kindly and well-intentioned I'm sure, that I join the senior citizens' group in town. I could barely hold back my tears. I thanked them for their suggestion and their hospitality, such as it was, and hurriedly left. Back home again I felt so defeated and desperate that I wished fervently that I would not awake to another day."

I was practically in tears. I had never imagined such devastating loneliness. Oh no, I thought. Here I am again, listening to his tales of woe. And yet I listened some more, trying to be supportive and, as hard as it was under the circumstances, optimistic. When I told him that I had to head back to my apartment in New York City, he asked me, almost pleadingly, "Can't you stay another day?"

Even if I could have stayed, I don't think I could have listened to one more depressing story coming from this man who, I could tell, was of superior intelligence, well-mannered, physically attracted to me (and, I suppose, I to him), and, in his own way, wanting to please me. Still, I wondered whether I could ever have a meaningful and fulfilling relationship with someone with such a doleful personality. Though like Fred, I too felt alone and lonesome for a companion, after that afternoon I wasn't even sure I wanted to see him again. He was the very opposite of the man to whom I had been married, a great conversationalist so full of life and humor and optimism, even in hard times.

I had been home only a short time when the phone rang. It was Fred. He was calling to find out if I had gotten home safely. It was a thoughtful and flattering gesture, but I wondered how much of it was a function of his own anxieties and fears and loneliness. After all, it had only been a 45-minute trip. However, the next night he called me, and the night after that. And for the next ten months he courted me. He told me that these phone calls were the highlight of his day. He had finally found someone he could have contact with on a daily basis.

Yes, I was lonely too. To have someone seemingly so devoted to me, so quickly, was pleasant and seductive. I looked forward to those calls. We'd usually talk about the personal events in our day, then go on to something that we had heard on the news. Within just a few days he was ending the conversation with, "Won't you please come up to Larchmont and have dinner with me?"

I was a traditional woman, believing that good girls don't run after boys. So I would answer, "You have to come down to my home first. Unless you want to keep this a telephone friendship only."

"Oh, nothing of the sort. If that's how it has to be, I'll come down to Manhattan," he told me.

But it was several months before that materialized. And when it finally did, I realized what an effort it must have been for him to come to me. It became obvious that he suffered from agoraphobia, not completely incapacitating him, but enough to make him fearful of leaving the safety of his home, especially by himself. It's possible that his fear was due mostly to his uneasiness about his health and what could happen to him when he was away from his medications and his physician.

Finally, after I had refused his invitation to Larchmont for at least the tenth time, he agreed to make arrangements to come to my apartment the following Saturday evening. He gave me all the details of his upcoming trip. He would take a private limousine down and back, and we would have an early dinner so he wouldn't get home too late.

I did want to see him again. Our phone conversations had become surprisingly lively and interesting. I was enthralled by his voice, which had a strong quality to it, and by his diction and his way with words. When he told a story, it was always well-told.

Saturday evening arrived and I found myself eagerly anticipating my date. I primped in front of the mirror, studying myself in a beige wool dress that, at the last minute, I decided to accessorize with a red paisley scarf caught at the neck by a pearl-and-gold pin. My blond— ok, bleached blond—hair was freshly coiffed.

And here he was. When I opened the door I saw a frail pale old man dressed in a dark coat, hat, and old-fashioned galoshes over his shoes, even though it wasn't raining. He was carrying a worn tan briefcase and a large black umbrella.

Was this the exciting date I had been expecting? Where was my Prince Charming?

As I took Fred's coat and hat and waited while he removed his rain shoes, I noticed that he looked pale and shaken and uncomfortable. I led him into the living room. He clutched his briefcase like a child with a security blanket. He sat down on the sofa with the briefcase at his side. I wondered what treasures it held. I had put out some wine, pâté, and cheese and crackers and offered him a drink.

"I'd like some orange juice, please," he said. "I have some in my flask in my briefcase but I'd like to keep that for my return trip."

How did I keep from laughing? The scene seemed so strange, so funny. Almost like a Woody Allen movie, I thought. I filled a cocktail glass with orange juice and ice. Make that two, I thought, and filled another glass with orange juice and ice for myself. Two bon vivants with our pre-dinner drinks!

After a few sips he asked to use the bathroom, and took his briefcase with him. I couldn't and didn't want to imagine why he was taking a rather long time. When he returned, he apologized.

"I had to change my undershirt and my shirt," he explained. "I had perspired so much on the ride down."

Cut and print that, Woody! Still, like the first time we met, I felt sorry for him and made an effort to be kind to him and put him at ease. We sat talking and drinking our respective OJ cocktails. When he looked at his watch, I realized that because of his diabetes he needed to make sure we left in time for him to eat at the proper time. I assumed he had a restaurant already picked out.

"Have you chosen a restaurant?" I asked him.

"No, I haven't," he replied. And then, to my amazement, he said, "Can we eat something simple here?"

I couldn't believe my ears. "I'm very sorry," I told him. "I'm really not prepared to eat in. I was expecting to be taken out for dinner."

Could I have said it any more clearly? You'd think he would have gotten it. Instead, he said, "Oh, anything will do, even a sandwich and a hot drink."

I wasn't budging. "No," I said. "There's a small restaurant just down the street, and even if it's raining, it's just a short walk."

Reluctantly he put on his rain shoes, his coat, his hat, and took his umbrella. I was surprised that he left his briefcase behind. What a despondent man, I thought. Why did I ever agree to see him again? Will I ever agree to see more of him? At the time I doubted it.

It was raining lightly as we walked to the restaurant. His large umbrella provided shelter for two and served us well. He gallantly held my arm as we crossed the street. Or maybe he was clinging to me for protection.

Once seated at the restaurant, he apologized. "I'm so sorry for having made a fuss. I'm so afraid of catching a cold and being unable to take care of myself."

I guess I could understand that, but at the moment, I was not having terribly kind thoughts. Surprisingly, our dinner went better than I had expected. Fred seemed to relax over his hamburger. We sat over our coffee for a long time, talking about ourselves. That's when I asked him, "Exactly what type of writing do you do?" And he replied, "Oh, I thought you knew. I write mystery stories."

"Under the name of Frederic Dannay?" I asked.

"No," he said. "Under the pseudonym of Ellery Queen."

Ellery Queen! I could hardly believe that this modest, unimpressive man could have been such a famous, world-renowned writer and well-known radio personality. I wondered why my friend hadn't told me. I suspected that it hadn't occurred to her to tell me since in her mind this man was simply going to be my dinner partner for one night only, not someone I would ever see again.

It dawned on me that when I was at his house I had noticed some small ceramic busts on a shelf and simply thought they were rather unpleasant-looking sculptures. It turned out they were busts of Edgar Allan Poe and prestigious awards for mystery writing.

"Why didn't you tell me before this?" I asked.

He had the answer. "Why should I have told you? Until now you had never asked what type of writing I did, so I didn't think you were interested, or that it was important to you."

There was nothing I could say in response. But it seemed, once Fred had revealed his true identity, he opened up about what he really loved to discuss the most: the mystery genre in all its details, the mystery writers, the pitfalls of the trade, and everything else associated with writing. The other topics of infinite pleasure were the art of collecting poetry, specifically English poetry, and, oh yes, stamps.

Fred did not have a college education. He had had to go to work immediately after graduation from high school because his family needed the money. He had such a natural curiosity and such a need to explore issues that interested him, together with his voracious reading, that these gave him a far greater education than college might have. He also had a keen and quick mind and an unusual native intelligence. He was a self-taught intellectual who gave the world the rewards of that mind through his mysteries.

We returned to my apartment and talked some more. Again, as in our phone conversations, I found myself responding to him and enjoying him, despite my initial impression when he first arrived. By the end of the evening he actually seemed energetic and, dare I say, happy.

"I don't know if you'll understand this," he said, "but I feel as if my death sentence has been commuted and a pardon is on its way."

"Just call me Governor," I said, trying to make a joke of it. But really, it made me feel uncomfortable.

His car service came promptly at 11p.m. I walked him to the door and he shook my hand. I had expected a kiss, on the cheek at least. And then he said, "Won't you please come to Larchmont next Saturday for dinner? I'll send a car for you."

I wasn't ready to say Yes but I wasn't ready to say No. So I said, "We'll be talking during the week, I'm sure. Let's wait and decide then."

I could see disappointment in his eyes. "Please come," he repeated. And then he was gone.

I had trouble sleeping that night. Too many conflicting thoughts ran through my mind, many similar to the ones I had thought about when we first met. I could appreciate how needy Fred was for companionship. I wanted a companion too. But could I be happy with someone who couldn't make me laugh? Was it possible for me to enjoy being around someone with no sense of humor? How much could I compromise?

Yes, I had found Fred interesting that night. And learning that he was a famous author was definitely exciting. Plus, he was so interesting, intellectual, mentally stimulating, when he wasn't being negative anyway. Those traits were important to me. And I told myself, "How can anyone know enough about another person in such a short period of time?" So when we talked during that week, I told him that I would see him again, on his terrain.

Saturday arrived and so did the car, at exactly 4 p.m. as Fred had suggested. He told me he wanted to allow time for talking and a short walk before dinner. As the car pulled up to Fred's house I could see him looking out one of the small side windows that flanked the front door. I would later learn from Hattie that whenever he expected me he would start waiting impatiently at the door long before my time of arrival.

When he opened the door for me, he took my hand and held it, I thought, for a few moments longer than the usual greeting required. I could feel his anxiety but also his pleasure in that handshake. I had bought a flower arrangement with me. He was surprised and a bit embarrassed.

"I owe you an apology," he told me.

"An apology?" I asked.

"Yes, for not having brought you something when I came to your home," he replied.

"Well, you didn't have to," I told him. "After all, I didn't give you any dinner. Not even the sandwich you asked for."

That made him smile, albeit sheepishly. Clearly he hadn't forgotten the initial events of that evening.

Hattie had put out the fine china reserved for special guests and the silver flatware atop an écru linen tablecloth with matching napkins. As we sat down, Fred announced, "I've planned the menu myself. I hope you like steak."

Fred seemed so much more relaxed in his own surroundings, and we both seemed ready to know more about each other. When dinner was over, topped off by Hattie's incredible homemade apple pie that Fred insisted on having with ice cream (diabetes be damned!), Fred suggested that we go to the living room so that Hattie could clean up and leave. I sensed his eagerness to have her leave as quickly as possible.

We sat at either end of the sofa, like two teen-agers waiting for the parents to go to bed. As soon as Hattie left, Fred timidly moved closer to me and reached for my hand. It was an endearing and romantic gesture, one that I had not anticipated. Holding hands seemed to inspire Fred to talk about his innermost feelings again, especially about his loneliness. How he enjoyed the idea of having someone next to him to talk to, someone to listen and sympathize! When my car arrived at exactly 11 p.m., it was difficult for Fred to let me go. He just clung to my hand and said, "Let him wait; he'll get an extra-large tip."

I was just about to leave when he presented me with two of his books. "This one is the gift I didn't give you when I visited you last week," he told me. "And this one is to show my appreciation for your coming here tonight." He repeated this gesture throughout our courtship. I was thrilled that first time and every time.

We stood at the front door and he embraced me tenderly. When he let me go, he looked at me beseechingly and made me promise that I would allow him to arrange for my return to Larchmont the following Saturday. I couldn't refuse, but I also couldn't help wondering, Am I doing this for him? Or am I doing it for myself?

His last words were: "I can't believe that in this short a time you've become so special to me."

Trying to define my own feelings, and having difficulty doing it, I nevertheless was amazed to find myself falling in love.

I was working during our courtship, so most of our time together was spent on Saturdays and Sundays only. I would stay over at my friend's house in Larchmont, the same house where we met. I was too "proper" to stay overnight at Fred's, even though I'm sure he would have agreed to my sleeping in the guest room. He didn't push me. I think he feared that he would lose me if he pressed the issue.

I had a month's summer vacation coming up, and Fred had a summer beach house on beautiful Fire Island. The house had been closed for the past few years because Fred had not wanted to be there alone. He asked me if I would consider spending a month there with him.

And I asked him, "My gosh, what would my mother say?"

I still remember the look of disbelief on his face. I'm not sure whether it was the look, or my sudden realization that I needed to take myself out of the Dark Ages (after all, I wasn't a 16-year-old virgin), but I burst out laughing, and so did he.

He had been telling me how much he loved me and how eager he was to marry me, but I was having some reservations about marrying him. There was his age, his diabetes, his tendency toward hypochondria, and the frightening fact that he had outlived three women younger than he. These tragedies involving the three women in his life, dying so painfully, weighed heavily on my mind. Was this a pattern in his life that would now involve me? Maybe I was being superstitious, but nevertheless it felt intimidating, and I needed more time to deliberate.

As it happened, before I met Fred I had made arrangements with two friends to go abroad for three weeks during the summer, so I couldn't accept his Fire Island invitation. Fred tried to coax me out of it and was unhappy when I refused to revise my plans. After all, my friends were counting on me. It would have been wrong to back out on my commitment to them. Besides, this would be a good opportunity to think more carefully and deliberately about my feelings.

I left my itinerary with Fred because I thought it would make him feel secure knowing exactly where I was. He could always reach me if necessary. And he did. At every destination a plaintively loving letter from him was waiting for me. I was flattered. After three weeks and six countries I was ready to go home. I missed Fred.

Our Life Together

Waiting for me at my front door was a huge basket of red roses, with a note: "Welcome home. Life has not been good without you." I ignored the glass-half-empty sentiment. I focused on the positive, the masterful stroke of endearment. A month later, on my birthday, he gave me a beautiful sapphire and gold ring and asked me to consider it as a part of our engagement pact. And then he said, "Let's visit your mother."

"Why now, Fred?" I asked.

"I want to ask her for your hand in marriage," he replied.

What a perfect old-fashioned gesture! I loved it. My mother loved it. My son and daughter thought it was slightly weird but, I think, endearing too.

My mother, widowed twice and alone for many years, was delighted that I was going to be married. She admitted that she had been worried about my being alone. It turned out that she had actually met Fred once before, years before I met him. His second wife's mother had been a friend of my mother and once, when Fred was visiting, my mother happened to be there. So she felt that she had a personal connection and considered him a great catch.

Without my knowledge, Fred had asked his son to prepare a prenuptial agreement for him. I was disturbed by it; it seemed so unromantic, so mercenary. I had no idea of Fred's finances. He had never volunteered the information and I had never asked. From his general situation, with a nice home, a car, a housekeeper and a gardener, I just assumed he was comfortable. And I was earning enough of a salary to make me feel quite independent. So why did we need a prenuptial agreement?

"Really," he told me. "It's customary for two people of our age."

"But to me it feels so crass, so undignified," I tried to explain. "It bespeaks less of love and more of distrust. I'm really shocked, and hurt."

But how could I turn away from him now? He was sincere. He loved me. He told me to have my attorney look it over and give me advice. I told him that I had no attorney but that I would find one in Larchmont. I really didn't comprehend how serious this was. My friend, the one who had introduced us, told me that she knew a retired lawyer who might do her a favor by looking it over. He agreed and she drove me to his home. He advised me not to sign it. Feeling shaken, I called Fred and told him what the lawyer had told me. Fred was furious. Almost shouting, he told me, "I don't care what he says. I'm a gentleman; my word is good. I love you, and I swear I will take care of you. You will want for nothing, now or ever."

I turned the phone over to the attorney. I could hear him saying, "I don't care what you're telling me. I must advise Rose against signing this."

After a few minutes he ended the conversation with, "She can do whatever she likes, of course, but I haven't changed my mind about advising her against it." Then he gave me the phone.

"You know I hate the whole idea of this," I told Fred. "But if you want me to sign it, I will, even against the lawyer's advice. And then I don't want to hear another word about it."

I hadn't realized that the document was just a copy, and I had to take an afternoon off from work to go with Fred to his son's office to sign the real thing. His son, flanked by several attorneys from his law firm, watched us sign. I was totally confused. Fred sat next to me, encouragingly holding and patting my hand, the hand that wasn't signing the documents. I was relieved when it was over. Fred kissed me. Everyone wished us luck and happiness. I went back to my office. Fred stayed behind. Once out the door I put the whole thing out of my mind. My thoughts were on all I had to do to finalize the wedding details: the place, the invitations, the menu and, most important, the dress. All this while I worked full-time. Fred had told me, "Whatever and however and wherever you want, dear. You don't need my approval for anything." Still, I would talk to him about it over the phone. He was always unconditionally encouraging. And I was very happy.

I dashed from store to store, looking for what I thought I wanted to wear. I finally found the perfect dress, a form-fitting, re-embroidered beige lace gown with soft but dramatic coq feathers at the wrist.

"Please come down and see it for yourself before I buy it," I implored Fred.

"No," he said. "I have implicit faith in your taste. Do anything you want; just come up to Larchmont early on Friday."

Yes, by this time I was spending the entire weekend at Fred's, and not in the guest room. But I didn't tell my mother!

Our wedding was held on November 11, 1975, on a clear sunny Sunday afternoon at the Plaza Hotel in New York City. But it almost didn't happen. The rabbi who was to marry us died suddenly of a heart attack. Oh no, I thought, is this an omen of things to come? Has Fred's curse not been lifted? The replacement rabbi was so young, ours was the first wedding ceremony he performed. At its conclusion he noted how pleased he was to be part of the festivities of an older couple who seemed so happy with each other.

After the reception Fred and I returned to Larchmont, escorted by his sister, who had come up for the wedding and was staying with us for one more night. A little embarrassing to spend our wedding night with a chaperone in our guest room! Fred and I tried to be discreet and quiet, though we were certain she would hear our teen-age giggling.

We postponed our honeymoon because I had to go back to work. We had just a few days together before I returned to my apartment, commuting to Larchmont at least four days a week. Fred stayed in Larchmont and worked from there. He called me at least once a day at my office and always in the evening when I got home from work. We hated being apart but I wanted to continue working for at least one year. I wanted to be sure our marriage would work before I resigned.

We only had a month to wait before we went on our 12-day honeymoon to the Caribbean Islands aboard the S.S. Rotterdam. I had never been to the Caribbean so each island we visited was sheer adventure for me. Onboard was fun too. The first evening, at dinner, we received an invitation to dine at the captain's table the following night.

The immediate response from our table mates was, "Now what famous personalities are you to receive the captain's invitation?"

I was absolutely bursting to tell them who Fred was, and Fred must have sensed it because he whispered to me, "Don't you dare say anything," and to our table mates he said, "I have no idea why we were invited."

Whenever possible he kept his identity hidden. That wasn't difficult. No one knew who Fred Dannay was. They only knew who Ellery Queen was.

Alas, neither Fred nor Ellery made it to the captain's table. That next morning Fred awoke with a terrible case of seasickness. The ship's doctor came to our cabin and gave Fred an injection. "This will make you feel much better," he told Fred. "You'll be up and around in just a few hours." He didn't know Fred. It took him two whole days more to recover. Meanwhile he just lay on his bed, feeling absolutely dreadful.

"Please don't stay with me," he insisted. "Go and have a good time."

So for two days I strolled along the deck by myself and sat in deck chairs reading a book, alone.

Fred also insisted that I honor the captain's dinner invitation. The captain and other guests were definitely cordial, but I had the feeling that they really wanted the pleasure of Ellery Queen's company. Well, so did I.

The next evening Fred accompanied me to dinner. Just as we sat down at our table, the Master of Ceremonies, a charming and witty young Irishman, approached Fred and whispered, "I've just been told by the captain who you are. Would you allow me to announce that Ellery Queen is sailing on this ship with us?"

Fred actually tried to deny who he was. Of course that didn't work, so he tried, "Please, we're just two ordinary people on vacation."

I pleaded with Fred. "I'm so proud of who you are; please let him make the announcement."

"No," Fred said, shaking his head. "Absolutely not."

"Well, I certainly don't want to be the cause of a lovers' quarrel," the Master of Ceremonies told us, and left to start the evening's program.

But that didn't stop me. I kept pleading with Fred until he finally said, "Oh, all right, Rose. Anything to please you, my pet." Or did he say "my pest"?

The Master of Ceremonies had been keeping his eye on us even while addressing the audience, and he must have sensed the sea change. In a flash he was at our side and, winking at me, said, "You won, didn't you?"

He returned to the stage and, before Fred could change his mind, he quickly made the announcement. It was the first time I had ever witnessed the overwhelming reaction of people upon learning they were in the presence of Ellery Queen. I thought it especially amusing because just before the announcement Fred had said to me, rather sharply, "Watch. You're going to be embarrassed when you see that nobody will even know who Ellery Queen is."

But then that was Fred, dubious about his own fame.

Our dinner companions were totally surprised and gave voice to their excitement and admiration. They all said that they had read and enjoyed his books.

And that wasn't all. When we had finished our dinner and were heading out of the dining room, Fred was stopped by dozens of people who told him how much they enjoyed his books.

"It's a pleasure being on the same boat with you," some said. Others told him, "Wait till we tell our friends who was on this ship!"

All that was the frosting on the cake for me. What really mattered to the two of us was the wonderful time we were having, just being together. My only anxiety during the trip was my concern for my mother, who had not been feeling well when we left New York. I had spoken to her right before we departed and I phoned her from several ports. I was happy to hear that she sounded somewhat stronger. Fred was very sympathetic, and that pleased me. When we disembarked, our car service was waiting for us at the dock, ready to take us back to Larchmont, but Fred suggested that we first go to visit my mother. What a loving and caring gesture that was, especially given that it was a real hardship for Fred to ride in a car for longer than absolutely necessary.

My mother was so surprised and thrilled. I noticed that she looked more frail than the last time I had seen her. We asked her about her health but she never complained. Instead she wanted to hear all about our trip. We hugged and kissed and left. I didn't realize that it would be our last farewell. She died in her sleep a few days later. It made me appreciate Fred's gesture even more.

When we returned from our honeymoon, we started a round of weekend entertaining, inviting our respective friends over to show each other off. Fred was like a little boy with a new toy, namely me. He sheepishly admitted that he wanted me to be admired and him to be envied. Fred's friends seemed to accept me warmly, and my friends were impressed with Fred's fame. But he wasn't easy to get to know. He was shy and had a tendency to listen rather than speak. Maybe that's a writer's trait. I had developed a system of coaxing him to talk by reminding him of something interesting he had told me in private. It worked very well and made Fred seem the social conversationalist he really wasn't.

Fred suffered through my weekly work absences for ten months. Finally he told me that he couldn't stand it any longer, that he was too lonesome during the day and too sleepless at night when I wasn't with him. Of course, I felt more content being with him in Larchmont than being alone in New York, so ten months after we were married, I gave up my job and became a suburban housewife.

I think I realized quickly that I could not be the typical suburbanite. I was unwilling and unable to hang around doing charity luncheons or playing bridge. I was used to walking in New York City, and I couldn't stand the thought of relying on a car in Larchmont, so I walked whenever and wherever I could. When people saw me, they thought something was wrong. I remember one particular time when I had just reached Byron Lane and walked by a woman spraying her rose bushes. She noticed me and called out, as most people did when they saw me walking, "Has your car broken down? Can I give you a lift?"

"Oh, no thank you," I replied. "My car is in the driveway. You'll probably think this is unusual, but I'm from New York City and taking walks is very common."

She laughed as I added, "And I love walking past all the beautiful gardens and homes along this street."

Then, coming closer to me, she lowered her voice and said confidentially, "Do you know who lives just up this street at number 29?" And before I had a chance to answer, she announced, "Ellery Queen, the famous mystery writer!"

I tried to think of a clever retort, but all I could say was, "Oh yes, I know that. I'm Mrs. Ellery Queen." No need to describe the expression on her face!

I had painted during my first marriage and had even taken some art classes. When I told Fred that I wanted to paint again, he helped me turn the smaller of the two guest rooms into a studio and encouraged me to start painting seriously. I soon joined a studio class held in a neighboring town and started a new career in a field I had always loved.

Before he started his writing career, Fred had been a copywriter and an art director for a New York City advertising agency. His cousin, Manny Lee, who would become his writing partner, worked for the publicity department of the Pathé movie studio. That was 1926. They were lucky to have jobs, no less good jobs. Good jobs weren't easy to find, especially if you were Jewish. In fact Fred changed his name from Daniel Nathan, combining the first letters from his first name with letters from his last name to create Dannay. Frederic came from the great Chopin, his favorite composer.

The cousins' offices were a short distance from each other so they usually met for lunch. They had been close growing up, and even as young boys they had shared a common interest in mystery stories. They had often talked about writing a detective novel together but it was all talk until the spring of 1928. That was when they read about a contest for a detective novel with a prize of $7,500, a lot of money in those days, sponsored by *McClure's* magazine and the publishing house of Frederick A. Stokes. Fred and Manny decided to enter. They had never even written a short story, but now they were going to write a novel. And even though Fred described it as a lark, they actually took it very seriously. They devoted all of their spare time to the project. And then some. In fact, so determined were they that once when Manny had to go to a wedding in Philadelphia, Fred went with him, to a wedding of total strangers, just so they wouldn't lose the time it would take Manny to get there and back.

When all that was left was coming up with a name for the main character, they decided to do something different, something that had never been done before. They gave both the detective and the author the same name, Ellery Queen. It evolved from their knowledge of advertising and promotion. The same name would mean that it would be easier to remember. But how did they choose the name? Ellery was the name of a childhood friend of Fred's. Queen was… They just liked the sound of the word.

They completed the manuscript the day before the deadline and hurriedly sent it off. Imagine their surprise and delight when they were informed they had won the contest! In their minds they began spending money. They envisioned themselves quitting their jobs and moving to Paris, the Left Bank of course, and leading writers' lives. Until…

They found out that *McClure's* had gone bankrupt. There would be no prize, or prize money. But Stokes was still in business, and its editors liked what they had read. They offered to publish it and agreed to pay them. Not $7,500, though. Not enough to get them to Paris. And thus began the writing careers of two cousins.

The Roman Hat Mystery was published in 1929. But the cousins didn't stop there. In 1931, despite bad economic times, they decided to quit their jobs and devote their full time to writing. The rest is history. And mystery.

The two men remained mysterious throughout their writing career. They wore masks when they appeared at speaking engagements. And they never divulged the mystery of who thought up the plots and who wrote the copy. Or did they take turns? The general consensus is that Fred thought up the plot and wrote a synopsis of about 25,000 words. Manny would then take over and flesh out the novel to about 100,000 words. Sounds easy, doesn't it?

What made the Ellery Queen novels different from other detective stories was that the authors played fair with the reader. Before the mystery was solved, the reader was told everything that the detective knew. Fred and Manny even offered a "Challenge to the Reader," a chance to solve the mystery before Ellery did. Besides the Ellery Queen mysteries, they wrote four novels under the name of Barnaby Ross.

In March 1953 *The Golden Summer* was published. Fred wrote this novel alone, under his birth name Daniel Nathan, an appropriate name because it was a story about his childhood, growing up in Elmira, New York. He told me that he wrote it as therapy while his son by his second wife was dying.

For Fred it wasn't just about writing, it was also about collecting. He collected and owned a copy of every volume of detective and crime short stories ever published.

It was around 1938 when Stokes published the first Ellery Queen anthology, *Challenge to the Reader*. It turned out to be a complete failure, an absolute bomb. Although the first printing was fairly small, it took Stokes years to sell those copies. Fred tried to analyze the reason for the failure and came to the conclusion that while readers like clever tricks in a mystery novel, they do not like them in an anthology. He started to think that the only sure-fire successful anthology had to be one of top quality.

He made up his mind that for his second anthology he would find the 50 best detective stories that had been published since Poe. He and Manny went down to the Library of Congress in Washington D.C. to do research for the new anthology, and to their horror they could find practically no books of detective fiction on the shelves of the Library.

That was when Fred decided to build his own library and started to collect the first editions of the best detective short stories ever put together. He solicited agents all over the world until he had acquired 6,000 books.

"The reading took a long time," Fred told me, "but finally I selected the 50 stories I wanted to use, made up a Table of Contents, wrote up a prospectus for the book, and sent the material to my agent."

His agent sent it to Stokes, who immediately refused the book. They had been burned once; they weren't going to risk it again. So Fred's agent sent it to other publishers, all of whom turned it down too.

Fred recalled, "I was discouraged, disappointed, disturbed. I thought about all the money that went into building that collection and all of the work involved in reading and deciding on the selection of stories."

And then two events occurred almost simultaneously. Stokes sold out to Lippincott, and Fred's agent gave up his literary agency work and became vice president of Little, Brown in Boston.

Over lunch one day the agent said to Fred, "Now that you have no publisher, would you consider joining Little, Brown?"

Fred pulled out of his pocket the prospectus for the anthology, which he always carried, and asked the agent, "Would you consider publishing it?"

"No, not in a hundred years," the agent replied. "It would be about a thousand pages and too expensive to publish, and you know the public doesn't care about anthologies."

About two weeks later the agent called and again asked Fred if he would come with Little, Brown.

Again Fred asked, "Would you consider publishing our anthology?"

Again the agent refused, and again Fred did not give him a definite answer.

The next time he called, Fred could tell he was desperate. "Fred, we're going to press in two weeks and we really want to list Ellery Queen as our author."

And Fred said, "Only if you publish our anthology."

According to Fred, the agent replied, "Damn it, yes, we'll publish it."

And Fred replied, "Ray, you've got yourself a new author."

The book was called *101 Years' Entertainment* and was eventually considered by the critics as the finest anthology of detective stories ever published in America. It remained in print for 35 years and became a Modern Library Giant.

As large as *101 Years' Entertainment* was, Fred still had many good stories left over, so he started using them in *Ellery Queen's Mystery Magazine*, which he edited from its inception until shortly before his death. It still exists!

Fred loved to tell me about the magazine, which he called his brain child, and how he had to fight hard to get it started. He and Manny had actually started a magazine in 1933 called *Mystery League*, which folded after four issues. With that failure, Manny wanted nothing to do with another magazine. "I don't want the work involved, and I don't want to go into anything that's bound to be a flop," he told Fred, but Fred still had his heart set on one.

He was sure it could have a future and he refused to be talked out of it.

Fred was always proud of the magazine, but especially proud when in about 1945 he started to publish stories of contemporary writers, with a "first story" by an unknown author in every issue.

In the years we were married, when Fred worked at home reading manuscript after manuscript, he would often threaten, "I'm going to retire. It's about time. I'm tired of reading and editing these stories day after day."

I knew better, for when I saw him read a story with what he called a twist in the plot, his eyes would light up as he eagerly read on, finishing it with a "Gosh, that's good" to himself, or to me if I were within earshot. I knew he enjoyed his work no matter how he complained and I knew he would never retire.

Fred had shown me his art portfolios and the graphic designs he had done for advertising clients. They were clever, innovative designs. So I loved it when he critiqued my artwork and I appreciated his input. He often suggested interesting additional touches to my paintings. He would always preface a suggestion with, "If you think it's feasible..." I can't remember any times when it wasn't. He had a very good eye for the unusual.

We led a quiet and loving life together, although I tried to arrange dinner parties as often as I could. We didn't go to the theater or concerts or museums as often as I would have liked. They simply presented too much effort for Fred, and I had to accept it. I'm sure that his desire to stay home above all else was connected to his concerns about his health. But he also feared that something would happen to him in public and that he would make a spectacle of himself. I had to assure and reassure him every time we went out that he would be fine.

I had learned from Hattie that Fred had had a habit of backing out of social engagements at the last minute. He'd be all dressed and ready to go when suddenly he would say that he was too sick to go. His wife would tearfully call their friends and say they couldn't come. I refused to follow that pattern. When he tried it with me, I would make him sit down with me. I'd take his hand in mine and assure him that he would be fine. Invariably, in his anxiety, he would perspire so much he'd have to change his shirt and his undershirt, just like on our first date in New York City. A little more coaxing with my arms around him and he would acknowledge that he was beginning to feel better. To Hattie's astonishment I would get him out the door. I'll always remember the subtle pat on the shoulder that Hattie would bestow on me as her sign of approval.

In fact Fred's health during our marriage was very good, as his periodic checkups indicated. His diabetes was controlled to the point that he only had to take an oral medication every other day. In the past, not only had he been required to give himself daily insulin injections, but he had also had to take his oral medications multiple times a day. He continued to carry his trusty, familiar briefcase everywhere, the briefcase that contained his flask of orange juice and sugar cubes in case his blood sugar level dropped. Every time he took a drink out of his flask, it reminded me of an alcoholic who couldn't wait for the party to begin. Once, when I had convinced him to drive into New York to see a play with some friends of mine, I noticed he was about to take his flask out during intermission, having no idea how it would look to people sitting around us.

"Can you wait until the lights go down?" I asked him.

"I won't be able to see then," he said as he threw his head back and tipped the flask. Glancing around surreptitiously, I noticed a woman shaking her head. Our eyes met and she said sympathetically, "It's not your fault, dear."

With great difficulty I contained my laughter and replied, "Thank you so much for understanding. This happens all the time."

It was a romantic marriage, which was surprising, I thought, given our ages. I never doubted that Fred loved me, but once, I remember, he quite unexpectedly took my hand, kissed it, and with tears in his eyes said, "Forgive me if I don't constantly tell you how much I love you, how happy I am with you. That's because I'm afraid you might be taken away from me." He said he felt unlucky, that the gods were not on his side, given the losses he had endured in his close relationships. For him it felt like a perfectly logical assumption after the deaths of his two wives, and the woman he was to marry, and his six-year-old son.

Perhaps to allay my own fears and to cheer him up, I said, "I've talked to your gods and learned that they've left town now that I'm here."

He smiled and hugged me hard, but I knew he didn't believe a word of what I said. Actually, throughout the years we were married, it was a constant effort to make him look at the sunny side of life, but I never gave up. He was always the man who saw the glass half empty. It was as if he felt that happiness was not intended for him, even though it was clear to me that he was enjoying life more now.

People used to say to me, "How lucky you are to be married to such a famous man," and I would reply, "How lucky that famous man is to be married to me."

Fred's collection of books of poetry was an endless source of wonder and enjoyment for me. I especially loved it when Fred relived the joy of his collection as he recounted the history of each book, how and where he had obtained it and how much it had cost. There were wonderful stories about his book dealer, the late Lew Feldman, and how Lew had helped him obtain some of his most precious books.

Lew knew Fred's collection and knew what Fred was looking for. When Lew attended an auction and purchased a fine book of poetry, he would call Fred and teasingly say, "I wonder if you would be interested in this first edition." Then he'd name a famous book of poetry, one that he knew Fred would be thrilled about, and Fred would answer, in a voice full of excitement, "You rascal, you know I'm interested. When can I have it?"

I met Lew when he delivered a famous book to Fred to our home. He was a tall dramatic-looking gentleman, who actually wore a black cape and a black fedora and carried a gold-headed walking stick. Except for the kind expression on his face, he resembled the villain in an old movie. He was an interesting man, and over lunch one day I listened to him and Fred animatedly discussing first editions of poetry and book collectors in general. On a rainy afternoon or a cold winter's evening, Fred and I would sit side-by-side in our living room, and Fred would lovingly pick one of his poetry books and read some of the poems to me. At times we would discuss the underlying meaning of lines, subject to interpretation, on which we did not necessarily agree. Still, it was a wonderful feeling of love and unity that these reading sessions brought to us.

Fred loved to hear me laugh, and right from the beginning he would take my hand, look at me pleadingly, and say. "Please don't ever stop laughing." He could understand humor but couldn't tell a funny story himself. In all our years together he rarely laughed out loud; the most he could do was smile broadly. It was indicative of his reserved personality and his negativity.

It was this negativity, and more, that in truth made him a difficult man to live with. He would lose his temper easily, without reason, and rant long and loudly until he provoked me to shout back. When he realized he had hurt me, he would stop shouting, say he wasn't feeling well, and stomp up to our bedroom and lie down. That was his way of calming down and regaining his composure. I would wait downstairs until he returned. And when he did, he would be meek and loving, as though nothing had happened.

Gradually I learned to predict the intensity of the outbursts, and when I noticed he was really losing control, I would say, quietly, "I'm going to go out until you're yourself again."

I'd go to the local library for an hour or so, or go shopping and buy myself something. When I'd drive into the driveway, I could see him peeking out through the curtained doorway window, relieved that I was home safely. He always worried that I was driving while I was upset, and I'm sure that with his vivid imagination he had me in dozens of dire situations while I was gone. Perhaps it was cruel of me to leave him at such times, knowing he would worry, but it was my way of self-preservation.

He was also an extremely suspicious person, turning the smallest incident into a veritable plot of intrigue against him. I was never able to counteract this behavior. I'd unsuccessfully try to tease or humor him out of it. Sometimes I'd just let him brood for a while. Sometimes I'd angrily tell him that life for him was always a conspiracy against him, and if he wanted to be morose and non-communicative, I'd have to absent myself. Again I'd get in the car and go off to the library or visit a friend or, yes, go shopping. Sometimes I'd just go up to my studio, close the door, and paint until Hattie called us for dinner. By dinner he was calm again. His suspicions usually involved someone at his office or his sons or one or another of his friends. The first time it involved me was in December 1976. My son and daughter and I had had a holiday tradition for many years which involved a Grab Bag that I would fill with little items, often useless and/or funny, that I had collected during the year. They would take turns reaching into the bag, ridiculing what they had picked and often trying to pawn it off on the other, or throw it back into the bag for next year.

Because Fred and I were going on our cruise and wouldn't be around for the holidays, I decided that I would put my silly knick-knacks in a Grab Box and send them to my daughter, who would be getting together with my son on Christmas day. As I was wrapping these gifts in the guest room, Fred came in, saw what I was doing, and asked, "Just what are you sending your children, and why have you not shown them to me?" I could hear the suspicion and anger in his voice.

"I guess I just didn't think you'd be interested in looking at junk," I replied.

"How do I know it's junk?" he asked.

Now I was feeling angry. "Because they're *my* junk," I told him. "But if you're, uh, suspicious…" Then I asked him, "Would you like to see whether any of these precious items are yours?"

He just stood there glaring at me, which made me more angry. I turned the box upside down on the bed, ripped off the wrappings, and said, "Now, make sure you examine them carefully." I was furious and horrified. Without another word I went downstairs, got into the car and drove off. This time I stayed away for several hours.

Hattie had the day off so Fred was home alone. He must have regretted his ugly outburst very soon after I left, and started panicking, because he called two of my friends to find out whether I was with them. I hardly wanted to return even after a few hours but, being the dutiful wife, I knew I had to prepare Fred's dinner on time. As usual Fred was at the door, contrite and wan-looking.

"I was worried about you," he told me. I knew that was his way of apologizing, but I was in no mood to accept such an off-handed approach. During dinner he tried to talk about what had happened, but I refused to discuss it. I merely said, "If you're convinced that there's nothing of yours in that box, I'd like to repack it as soon as I'm finished with dinner."

The next day I received roses from the florist and a box of chocolates. Fred was not able to apologize, quite incapable of admitting to being wrong. He tried to make amends in circuitous but effective ways. I couldn't remain angry with him or uncommunicative. It wasn't in my nature. And I suppose the upheaval worked to my advantage. He never doubted my word again, nor did he ever play Mystery Story with me again.

That Fred could write an interesting story is a foregone conclusion, but during the years we were married he recounted many things that had happened to him during his lifetime so interestingly, so vividly, that I could picture the whole incident as if it were happening as he spoke.

One of the most frightening episodes was an automobile accident in 1940. He was driving a big new beautiful Buick for the first and last time. Fred said that he never again bought or drove a Buick, even though the accident had nothing to do with the brand of car. As he told it, he was driving to Long Island to visit his mother and was just approaching an underpass when a car without lights, driven by a drunk driver, suddenly appeared out of the darkness and hit Fred's car head-on. The car was crushed against a cement wall and totaled, so much so that the only recognizable part was one of the wheels which had flown off on impact.

Fred would never know who witnessed the accident, who called for help, but the police and an ambulance from a nearby hospital arrived quickly. When they lifted this unconscious, crushed and bloodied body from the wreckage, the medics didn't stop to give him first aid. They just put him into the ambulance and sped off to the hospital. The ambulance driver later said that he thought Fred was a hopeless case, and his aim was to get him to the hospital where, he assumed, Fred would be pronounced dead. There seemed to be no signs of life. Fred believed that because they didn't stop to try to revive or treat him, they probably saved his life.

Fred's identification was found at the scene. Someone took pictures of the wreck and sent the report to the nearest newspaper that the only occupant of the car was apparently dead. After all, given the condition of the car, who could have survived?

As Fred lay in the emergency room, being worked on frantically by the doctors, Walter Winchell, who had a national radio program, came on the air with his "Good evening, Mr. & Mrs. America." And then, "Dreadful news tonight. Mystery writer Frederic Dannay, one-half of the Ellery Queen team, has just been killed in a terrible auto accident in Long Island."

Imagine the effect of Fred's family and friends listening to that program that night!

Fred was in the hospital for months, hanging onto life by the proverbial thread. He must have been physically stronger than he imagined, for against all odds he recovered fully.

All Fred was able to find out about the other driver was that he was unhurt, a young soldier, A.W.O.L., driving drunk without a license or insurance. Fred never sued him.

Fred told me stories about his radio days. He always considered the show *Author! Author!*, which he and his cousin had created in 1939, as one of the most fascinating experiments in radio.

The program would start with a brief dramatization of some unusual event. Here's an example: A customer in a jewelry store offers the salesman $1.00 for a watch worth $1,000. The clerk of course refuses and calls the manager, who immediately accepts the dollar payment. At such a point the moderator would challenge the four panelists, Fred and Manny and two famous guests—Ogden Nash, for example, and S.J. Perelman, Dorothy Parker, Moss Hart, George S. Kaufman, Mark Van Doren, Fannie Hurst, Heywood Broun, among others—to come up with the solution to this scenario and their versions of "why?"

Everyone seemed to have a great time arguing as to whose solution was correct. It was a coast-to-coast broadcast, and Fred and Manny received many letters from listeners saying how much they enjoyed the program. However, after about six months the show was cancelled. Fred told me that he could not understand why.

Not to be deterred, in June of 1939 they again started a radio program on CBS, this time with a one-hour script. *The Adventures of Ellery Queen* was the first hour-long dramatic mystery show in the history of radio.

Fred was so happy when I told him that I remembered listening to the show and looking forward to it each week. For about four months the program was on air without a sponsor, and it looked as if this show might be cancelled too. Here too each episode would be interrupted and the listener would be challenged to solve it. Each week there was at least one distinguished guest who would be the amateur detective and attempt to pinpoint the murderer before Ellery Queen would give the correct solution. Two of the early guests were Lillian Hellman, the playwright, and Margaret Bourke-White, the photographer.

One evening, just about 10 minutes before the end of the show, something happened to the transmitter system in the Chicago station, WBBM, and the program went off the air. The radio station received thousands of calls from listeners asking to be told the identity of the murderer, which proved beyond any doubt that the program was being heard by a very large and enthusiastic audience. Everyone connected with the show was accused of having done this deliberately as a brilliant publicity move. But Fred liked to say, "No, it really was an act of God." The best part of the incident was that it attracted the attention of Gulf Oil, which immediately became the sponsor.

The show lasted for nine years, eventually being sponsored by Anacin and Bromo-Seltzer. Until the final illness of Fred's first wife, all the scripts were written by Fred and Manny, which was a tremendous work load for them, but it was rewarding emotionally and monetarily, and it gave a new dimension to their creative minds.

Fred told me two stories about the actors who played Ellery Queen on the show. One was about Hugh Marlowe, who Fred felt was the best interpreter of Ellery on radio. Marlowe so closely identified himself with his role that he sometimes lost track of the distinction between himself and the character. One month Fred and Manny were shocked to receive statements from several department stores for a number of suits, shirts, and shoes, all charged to Ellery Queen. Knowing that neither one of them had purchased these articles, they called the stores and learned that a man calling himself Ellery Queen had opened the charge accounts. Upon further investigation they found that Marlowe had stepped over the line of playing the role and had come to think of himself as Ellery Queen. He had no intention of not paying those bills, which of course he did. In telling the story, Fred said with a mischievous twinkle in his eyes, "I wonder if he actually had his shirts and handkerchiefs monogrammed E.Q." Fred learned later that Marlowe had even been around town looking for a murder so he could solve it.

It is hard to believe that something like that would happen again, but it did, this time with another actor. Sydney Smith, one of the performers who played the role after Marlowe. One day Manny's wife, Kaye, happened to be at Carnegie Hall and saw a billboard that Ellery

Queen was to speak to a group of children on Crime Does Not Pay. Kaye went home and asked Manny if he was appearing and he said "No". He checked with Fred and Fred said "No". They eventually found out that it was Sydney Smith who was appearing that day. After the lecture they admonished Smith that he could not play Ellery Queen except on their program. I laughed as Fred continued and said that Smith was amazed and actually seemed resentful at their attitude. He told Fred that he thought he had done Ellery Queen a good deed by generating the extra publicity.

Fred also had lots of stories to tell about his time in Hollywood.

When in the late 1930s he and Manny went to Hollywood to work for Columbia, and then M.G.M. and Paramount, they found that Hollywood was not as glamorous as they had expected. Their stories never gained any screen credits. Fred would say, "We were paid very well, but neither of us took any satisfaction from what we produced."

According to Fred, they couldn't get any satisfaction after hours either. The writers were not a friendly group and seemed to think of each other as competitors. Still, Fred had some humorous incidents to recount.

His encounter with a famous producer gave Fred a startling experience and me a good laugh. Fred received a call to come and see this man at his apartment to talk about a storyline.

Fred asked, "Shall I bring my partner?"

"No, it's not necessary," he was told.

Fred arrived promptly at the required time, rang the doorbell, and waited for someone to come to the door.

Instead a cheerful voice shouted, "Come in, the door's open, Ellery."

Fred walked into a beautifully furnished living room in a lavish penthouse apartment, with no one in sight. Then the voice again. "I'm in here."

"Here," Fred was to discover, was a bedroom, almost completely mirrored, with dimmed lights, and there on the bed lay the famous producer, completely disrobed.

"So glad you could make it," he told Fred, who took one more glance around, quickly solved the mystery of why he had been invited solo, said "Good night," and left.

"Perhaps it was our last name 'Queen' that got me into trouble," Fred quipped.

Another interesting story was about the time the cousins had been hired by Paramount. They were given a small office in the building. From the day they arrived, none of the other writers talked to them or even invited them to sit at the same table in the cafeteria with them. Fred and Manny continued to chalk it up to rivalry. Weeks went by and Fred and Manny remained isolated, having no one but each other to talk to.

"And then one Saturday night, we were sitting at a table at a place called The Pig and Whistle, with no idea of what to do," Fred recounted. "We had seen every movie within miles of Hollywood and we were sitting there feeling pretty dejected and sorry for ourselves."

Suddenly one of the writers came over to their table, and asked, "What are you guys doing tonight?"

"Nothing," they answered, perhaps too quickly.

"Well, some of the boys down in Los Angeles are having a poker game. Would you like to join us?"

Fred and Manny knew it was dangerous to join a card game with people they didn't know but, Fred reiterated, they were absolutely desperate for human contact.

They arrived at a very elegant apartment house which immediately made Fred uneasy. Sitting around a table were six men in their shirt sleeves, engrossed in their game.

There were introductions all around. The actor Frederic March was there. So was the actor Ralph Morgan, and the production head of Selznick International, and three other bigwigs in the industry.

As Fred and Manny were settling in, someone asked March what he was working on.

"Oh," he said, "I've just been offered $125,000 for each of four pictures. I'm deciding whether to take it."

The Selznick man immediately counseled, "Stall. Don't do anything at all. They'll raise it to $150,000."

Then someone asked Ralph Morgan, "Have you seen your brother Frank recently?"

And he replied, "Oh, sure, we were just together [on a famous director's yacht]. We played poker all weekend."

"How did Frank make out?" someone else asked.

"He lost $40,000."

Fred looked at Manny and knew exactly what he was thinking. Fred was thinking the same thing: "Boy, are we in the wrong place."

The Selznick man, who was the banker, handed them chips, saying, "The blues are 25, the reds ten, and the whites are five."

They were playing seven-card stud, a wild poker game that the six men played more wildly than Fred and Manny had ever seen. The cousins watched for a few minutes as the players raised and re-raised their bets with abandon.

Thinking about Frederic March holding out for more than half a million dollars for four pictures, and Frank Morgan losing $40,000 at a recent game, Fred was petrified to imagine what was going to happen to him and Manny. Somehow, by playing conservatively, they managed to get by with a loss in the low 300s, just $320 or $340, or so they thought.

It was 3 a.m. when Frederic March finally said, "I've had about enough. How about closing up?"

"You boys want to pay up?" the Selznick man asked them.

Fred replied, "I'm sorry, I don't carry that much cash with me. Will you take a check?"

"A check?"

And Fred thought, "You mean they don't even trust me enough to take my check."

"A check?" the banker repeated. "For $3.40?"

When I think back over our eight years of marriage, there are experiences that hold a special place in my heart.

One of them took place on October 3, 1981 on the occasion of a black tie affair held at Bloomingdales in Chestnut Hill, Massachusetts on behalf of the Robert F. Kennedy Action Corps, a non-profit agency for troubled children. We had been invited by my son-in-law, the agency's Executive Director. Among the honored guests besides Fred who had been invited were Senator Ted Kennedy, his sister Pat Kennedy Lawford and her children Sydney and Christopher, Marvin Traub, Chairman of the Board of Bloomingdales, and Massachusetts Lieutenant Governor Tom O'Neill.

As usual I had a hard time convincing Fred to attend. My

daughter appealed to Fred's good nature by telling him it was for a worthy cause. Finally Fred consented.

It truly was a gala event. When introductions were made of the well-known people there (unfortunately Ted Kennedy wasn't able to make it), everyone received a polite round of applause. But when Fred, who was saved for last, was introduced, there was a perceptible gasp in the audience and a noticeable acceleration of applause.

The applause died down and within seconds, it seemed, Pat Kennedy Lawford came over to Fred to tell him, "Teddy will be absolutely devastated when I tell him that he missed meeting you. He is an avid fan!"

She asked Fred to autograph her program and then said, "Don't go away. I'll be right back." And sure enough, in a minute or so she returned with her daughter Sydney and a photographer to take their picture with Fred. She promised to send us a copy, and she did. I loved it. So did Fred, standing between two beautiful women towering over him. He was beaming.

I also have special memories of the time a Japanese television crew came to our home in Larchmont. Fred had accepted the invitations to do several introductions to Japanese TV mystery stories. Some of the filming was done in Manhattan in a hotel room on Central Park South, with Fred seated at a desk, giving his analysis of the story to be televised. But in Larchmont Fred sat in the living room in an easy chair. He reminded me of Alistair Cooke.

We received tapes of these mystery stories with Fred's introductions dubbed. How Fred and I laughed, seeing him on our television speaking fluent Japanese!

I remember one "Thank You" speech that Fred gave in Japan at one of the many banquets honoring us.

Naming many of our hosts and stating specifically how we would remember each one, he added, "And all others who have been so warm, so cordial, so generous that it is beyond my ability to describe.

"Our visit to Japan is like a poem. I am reminded of a great English poet, William Wordsworth, who spoke of poetry as 'recollection in tranquillity.'

"Not until after we return home will my wife and I realize the full beauty of our visit, of Japan, and of all the people we met. Only later will we recollect in tranquillity all the beauty of our visit."

He ended with a Haiku poem that he had written for the occasion:

Two Americans
Dropped from the sky to Japan
And their love blossomed.

I not only remember Fred's incredible collection of poetry written by famous poets, but I also and perhaps more personally remember the poems that Fred had written, beautiful poetry which, to his disappointment, had never been published. Publishers felt that the poetry was too personal and would not be a marketable item.

Fred loved to read these poems to me.

He would ask, "Do you like it? Is the meaning clear, not ambiguous?"

We had many discussions about these poems. At times he would ask me if I thought he should change a line, as if I could ever do better than he. They were beautiful poems; personal, yes, but that made them dearer to me.

On our fifth wedding anniversary he presented these poems to me in book form, together with a sentimental anniversary card on which he had written, "For you, dear, for the happiness you have given me."

I recall a unique experience Fred and I had one evening. Even now, when I think about it, I still can't believe that Fred got us into it.

A young woman, describing herself as a freelance writer for a Westchester magazine, had called Fred several times and asked for an interview. Each time Fred put her off, sometimes saying he was busy, which most often he was, and sometimes simply saying No, because he was such a private person.

Finally he succumbed to her pleading. And she suggested that we come to her home where she would prepare a light dinner and interview Fred. She and her husband would pick us up, she told him, and bring us home, at any time on any day we chose. To this day I have never figured out what caused him to agree to this in the first place. Fred picked a time and date, suggesting we would come in the early evening.

It was during the winter and it grew dark outside early. Our doorbell rang and there on our doorstep stood a tall blond man who, with a German accent, introduced himself as Cheryl's husband, Peter.

"Where is Cheryl? Didn't she come with you?" Fred asked.

"No, she decided to stay home and finish last minute cooking," he replied.

We got into his car with some trepidation. Fred and I were sitting together in the back seat, and as the car went from one dirt road to another, one road darker than the last, without a house or street light on it, Fred's hand tightened on mine as he whispered, "I don't like this ride." I knew exactly what he meant.

"Do you think we're being kidnapped?" I whispered back.

Fred had conceived another, more involved plot. "I hope our house isn't being broken into," he replied, thinking we were being taken away from home because someone wanted to burglarize it.

Suddenly the car slowed down.

"Well, here we are," said Peter. "It will be easier if we go around to the rear of the house."

"Don't you even let your company come in the front lighted entrance?" I jested.

Fred's hand tightened on mine once more, as though to say "Don't antagonize the perp."

Everything was pitch-black. We half-expected a dark cave to open up, but the garage door went up slowly, and we saw the lighted interior, though not a soul in sight.

How strange, I thought. After pursuing Fred for so long, this woman would not make it her business to be waiting for us.

Peter honked his horn twice. A signal of some kind? Then a door opened, and there stood a pretty young woman who we were right to assume was Cheryl. All smiles, she rushed out to greet us. "How happy I am to meet you in person," she exclaimed. "Please come in."

We had a lovely evening, a delicious dinner, and Cheryl had her interview. But we discovered that there was an ulterior motive. It turned out that the two of them were mystery writers, she a professional and he just starting out. They had written two mystery stories which they asked Fred to read. Fred, always looking for first stories to publish in *Ellery Queen's Mystery Magazine*, took the stories home with us. Actually they were good, and Fred did publish them both, back to back. So this adventure had a happy ending all around, though with Fred's suspicious mind, developed over years of writing mysteries, I think he didn't even trust the pleasant outcome of the evening until we reached home safely that night. And Fred did receive a copy of the magazine interview.

Fred always wrote an introduction to each story in *EQMM*, and when he told the unusual incident that preceded the publication of these stories, one reader wrote in a tone that could have easily be construed as angry, "So is that the way to be published? Invite the editor to dinner?"

Summers on Fire Island

We'd spend eight months in Larchmont and four months on Fire Island where Fred had a wonderful summer home. I had never been to Fire Island but I knew how unique and special it was. It could only be reached by ferry; no cars were allowed; it was bounded by ocean on one side and bay on the other.

Even so, Fred was so worried that I wouldn't like it. He knew that I wasn't a beach person. I preferred trees, grass and mountains to sun, sand and water.

He kept saying to me that first year, "We'll go to the beach in June for just a weekend, and if you don't like it, we need not keep the house."

"You mean you'd actually sell it?" I asked him.

"Yes," he replied. "I'd actually sell it."

On a sunny weekend in June we headed to Fire Island. As we stepped off the ferry and I surveyed my new surroundings, Fred asked eagerly, "What do you think? What do you think?"

"This is fantastic," I said. The invigorating air on the half-hour ferry ride; the cleanliness and peacefulness of the island that were immediately evident; the idea of no cars; little wagons, mostly red, lined up along a fence at the dock, waiting for their owners to load them up and take them for their walk home; the sound of birds chirping merrily; the natural beauty that was everywhere. This was as close as it came to my idea of paradise. And I knew it immediately.

Fred led me to his two red wagons and we piled them up with the clothes, books and groceries we had brought with us from Larchmont. Fred's house was about nine blocks from the dock. Along the way Fred kept imploring, "Do you really like it?"

"I love it; I absolutely love it," I assured him, my eyes darting from one incredible vista to another. Fred's house was marvelous too. There were two bedrooms, two bathrooms, Fred's study, a large open living room with a dining area and a dining table big enough to seat eight comfortably, and a thoroughly modern and functional kitchen right down to the dishwasher.

I was absolutely ecstatic and went from one room to the next, making happy little noises, then rushing outdoors to re-visit what I loved best right from day one: the two large decks, one at the front of the house and one at the side, from which I could see the blueberry bushes, pine trees, beach plum bushes and holly trees. It looked as though there were birds' nests in almost every one of them. And, would you believe, I even saw a young deer walking slowly across the street.

"Did you order her from Hollywood casting especially for me?" I asked Fred, who was standing by my side. He was so pleased by my enthusiasm that he took me in his arms and said, "I can't begin to tell you how happy I am that you like it here."

I believe Fred was not only pleased that I loved Fire Island so much. He was also pleased that without a car, without my job, without art classes or clothes shopping, we would be that much more isolated and dependent on each other's company. But I could still paint, especially outdoors, and he could still edit the magazine. And I felt so happy to be with him. It didn't matter where we were. People in the community were a lot more dependent on each other too, especially for entertainment. There were few restaurants and only one movie theater. Fred had friends here whom I had never met. Word of our arrival had spread, and everyone seemed eager to meet Fred's new bride. We had hardly unpacked when the phone rang and we were invited to dinner at the home of the neighbors across the street. Fred was happy to accept. He felt indebted to these neighbors because after Fred's second wife's death, when Fred tried to stay alone at Fire Island, they had been extremely solicitous of him. Still, it hadn't worked out. He had returned to Larchmont after only a few weeks.

Before we knew it, we were engulfed in a social round-robin with a group of very interesting people, even though Fred admitted to being torn between being by ourselves and showing me off. In general, though, he seemed to be much more social and much more relaxed. But his dark side showed up here too.

It all started when the electricity went out and stayed out for almost 24 hours, long enough for all our food in our refrigerator to go bad. When the power came back on, Fred suggested that we go out for dinner. Though we often biked to the restaurant, Fred decided that we would walk. We chose a restaurant that specialized in seafood. Fred and I usually ordered a fish dish but that night I decided on a hamburger. I took one bite and realized the meat was no good. "It has a sour taste," I told Fred. "I bet it's been here overnight without refrigeration. Please get the waitress's attention and tell her."

"Don't you dare say anything," he told me. "Just order something else."

Of course I had been aware that he was so afraid of doing anything in public that might call attention to himself. Sometimes I thought that, being a well-known personality, he was afraid it would bring him unfavorable publicity, but I was sure that no one in this restaurant had any idea who he was. So I wondered whether he thought that complaining might make him appear to want something for free, and then he would appear to be cheap.

"That's not the point," I tried to explain. "They need to know so they don't serve the meat to anyone else."

He glowered at me as he said, "Don't make a scene. Just order something else."

I pushed the envelope. "How will I make a scene if I just tell the waitress quietly?"

He didn't say anything, but the expression on his face didn't change.

"Never mind," I said. "I'll just eat the potato and vegetable. I don't think I'm feeling very hungry anymore."

After Fred paid the check to the cashier, who was also the owner of the restaurant, I said to her, quietly, "Please taste your hamburger meat before it's served again. I think it has gone bad, probably because of the power outage last night." She thanked me in what seemed to me an appreciative tone.

As soon as we were out the door, Fred started shouting at me. "You broke your promise; you told her about your dinner when I specifically told you not to."

And I responded, "You told me not to say anything to the waitress, and I didn't. You told me not to cause a scene, and I didn't. But I considered it my civic duty to tell the owner."

But he wouldn't stop shouting at me.

Finally I said, "If you don't stop shouting, I absolutely won't walk home with you." But that didn't stop him. So I turned off the main road at the first corner I came to. By the time I got home, Fred was there, seemingly engrossed in a book. As our bedtime approached, I asked, as I always did, what he would like for a snack. This time he didn't answer. We went to bed in silence, and the next morning, when I served him his breakfast, he was still not talking to me. The silence continued through lunch. And even though I tried a couple of times to engage in conversation, he would not respond. This went on for two more days until I couldn't stand it any longer.

"Fred," I finally said, "I'm going back to Larchmont tomorrow morning. If you want to remain silent, then you can remain silent alone."

I had never had an experience like this, and I was terribly unhappy. The next morning I awoke early, went to town to pick up the mail and, would you believe, actually bought a few frozen dinners for Fred. When I returned to the house, there was Fred waiting for me at the corner. He started to tell me that he had gotten a call from his office. I pretended not to listen. I was waiting for an apology, even though I knew that that was something Fred could never do. His way of making amends was to pretend that it never happened and send me flowers. Once again he was following his usual pattern.

"I know this is your way of telling me that you're sorry," I told him. "And it's totally inadequate. But I understand you so I'll accept it." I paused for a moment to let it sink in, and then I added, "I swear to you I will never tolerate anything like this again. The next time you pull this silent treatment on me, I will leave immediately. I will never let you make me as unhappy again as I've been these past few days."

He just stood there. He had tears in his eyes but he couldn't say he was sorry. Still, he never tried that tactic again.

After Fred's death his sister told me that even as a child he had

had a temper that he wasn't always able to control. He had so hidden it from me before we married. I wondered, had I known, would I have still married him? I think the answer is yes. Had someone told me about this trait ahead of time, I probably never would have believed it. He was so kind and considerate throughout our courtship. And throughout our marriage, there were all the wonderful times that I will always cherish.

Fred told me early in our relationship that as a child he had had nightmares and, worse, walked in his sleep. His mother was told by their family doctor to place wet towels on the floor around his bed so that if he got out of bed to sleepwalk, the wet cold towels would wake him.

"Did it help? Or was that the way your mom got you to wash the soles of your feet?" I had once asked him. He overlooked my attempt at humor.

"No, no," he replied seriously. "It really worked, but occasionally I think my mother forgot the towels, and I'd actually take my nocturnal walk."

It never occurred to me to ask if those childhood walks or nightmares were still with him. Luckily for him, I didn't know. The sleepwalking was gone but the nightmares weren't. It's lucky I loved him because soon after our marriage I found out that Fred still had them.

When Fred was on *The Dick Cavett Show* in 1978, he mentioned that one of the things he wanted to be was an actor. Well, truly, had Fred really pursued it, he would have needed no Method acting lessons. No actor could have done those nightmare scenes better than he. Suddenly in the middle of the night he would spring upright in bed and, with a booming voice that could easily have filled a large auditorium, he would shout, "Watch out! He's got a gun! He's coming at us!"

Can you imagine my panic the first time this happened? My racing heart, my fright? Oh, how dreadful it was being wakened out of my sleep that way! I never got used to it, no matter how hard I tried.

It wasn't easy to wake Fred or control him. He was usually still half-asleep and shivering with fright. When finally he realized what had happened, he would be so apologetic, so contrite.

"Oh, I'm so sorry," he'd say. "How can I make it up to you for frightening you so?"

How indeed? He certainly hadn't meant to do it. I often wondered whether I could have died of shock. After Fred calmed down, he could go back to sleep again. But I'd be lying there wide awake for what seemed like hours.

I remember one of his worst nightmares. It happened on Fire Island. Our twin beds were separated by a small night table which had a lamp on it. One night, in his nightmare state, shouting, "He's after me! I've got to get away!" he jumped off his bed, tried to jump over mine, knocked the lamp off the table and fell to the floor between our beds. He landed with such a resounding thud that I thought he had surely broken some bones. But when he pulled himself up, we discovered that he had only a few minor bruises. After that episode I put our beds together. Not that it stopped his nightmares, but it did at least prevent him from falling to the floor.

When my sense of humor returned, certainly not that night or the next morning, I asked Fred if their family doctor had ever advised his mother to put a wet gag in his mouth. Not seeing the humor in it, Fred asked seriously, "Do you think it would help?"

HELP!

A Trip to California

It was September 1977. The University of California at San Diego, which housed a Mystery Library, was developing a course in mystery fiction, and John Ball, the author of *In the Heat of the Night* and the acting chairman of the library's editorial board, had put together a three-day conference. The agenda included deciding which classic mysteries should be reprinted as Mystery Library selections, reviewing the course, and considering the possibility of working with the Corporation for Public Broadcasting on a 13-part series dedicated to American mystery fiction. An article about the conference in the Los Angeles *Times* Book Review was titled "Mystery Genre Gets Literary Status Boost."

The list of attendees boasted 25 of the most successful mystery writers, editors, critics, agents, producers and publishers in the world. Fred was on the list, and rightly so. If I may quote Elliot Gilbert, University of California professor, author and anthologist: "Fred Dannay is the most influential figure in the world of detective fiction today. In his role as editor of the world's foremost mystery magazine, he has published every major writer who ever produced a mystery short story, and has also given almost 500 mystery writers their first chance to be published."

About his accepting the invitation to attend, Fred would say, "John [Ball] begged, insisted, coerced, and in a weak moment I agreed."

Besides attending the meetings, Fred conducted question and answer sessions for faculty, students and his contemporaries, so that he wouldn't have to give lectures. He also signed autographs. Given Fred's reputation for privacy, someone had decided that we should be housed in an off-campus cottage, while everyone else was housed in on-campus dormitories. It was a very nice gesture but we did feel isolated. There was no phone in the cottage, and cell phones didn't yet exist, so I worried. In case of an emergency, what would I do? I didn't say anything about my concern to Fred, of course, and luckily there was never a need to answer that question. Arrangements had been made for a small tram and driver to take us to meals and meetings and back to the cottage whenever we desired. I don't remember having to walk anywhere. In fact, I said to Fred, "We need only be able to walk from the bathroom to our bed at night and reverse the process in the morning." That made him smile.

Early in the conference, Fred answered some questions from a San Diego television reporter who seemed to believe that the mystery story was less than worthy literature. Addressing Fred as Mr. Queen, he asked, "Do you think this college course on the mystery story will lend dignity to the mystery?"

Fred: "I certainly hope that it will. The backing of the university is tremendously important in impressing the public and particularly the critics."

Reporter: "Is the higher status deserved?"

Fred: "Not only that, but late in coming."

Reporter: "Why does the mystery deserve to be called first class literature? Isn't it just escapist fare?"

Fred: "Well, it is entertainment. But what's wrong with entertainment? Do you consider show business worthy of second-class citizenship?"

Reporter: "They don't make college courses about it."

Fred: "Oh, there are a great many courses on film and theater."

Reporter: "Then why do you suppose the mystery novel has had second-class status for so long?"

Fred: "You might ask that of ethnic groups as well. May I ask you a question? Do you read mystery stories?"

Reporter: "I don't. I've never read an Ellery Queen novel. I guess I'm a case of arrested development. I stopped after Sherlock Holmes."

Fred: "That was a good place to start, not to stop. The detective story has developed tremendously since Sherlock Holmes. No one can deny Holmes' importance. He's probably the best-known literary character in all history. But a lot has happened to times, to cultures, to the way we live and think. We're reflecting what's happening in the world in 1977. This Sherlock Holmes couldn't do. He did, however, reflect Victorian England better than any so-called serious work of the time."

Reporter: "In all fairness, I should say that I don't read novels either."

Fred: "You certainly were the right reporter for this job!"

The audience broke into laughter and applause for Fred, who had succinctly and cleverly put this brash young man in his place.

Incidents like this made my heart skip a beat with pride. Fred was so clever, and if I was sitting next to him, in full view of everyone I would lean over and kiss him. In full view of everyone, this shy man would kiss me back.

One of the largest panel discussions held during the conference was one attended by all of the writers, faculty, their guests, students, and even some friends and relatives of mine who had read about the event in their local newspapers. It was a packed house. Much to my surprise, Fred had agreed to speak before the session. He had asked for a large blackboard and chalk because he had decided to do a visual experiment in explaining the short story. What he called the EKG of a short story. But first he gave his definition of a short story: "A short story is a story that's not long." That was Fred making a joke!

"In Edgar Allan Poe's time," he continued, "ten thousand words was considered a short story. Today, a short short story is fifteen hundred words; a short story is usually four to six thousand words; ten to twelve thousand words is now called a novelette or novella; twenty thousand words is a short novel; and fifty thousand words is a novel. All these figures are dependent on the customs of the times."

Then he went to the blackboard, drew a long horizontal line, and said, "This story shows no mounting sense of excitement. In medical terms, this story is dead." He proceeded to draw a series of other lines, horizontal, vertical, oblique, descending, ascending, and gave explanations for all of them. Some of these were very funny. I know it may seem like a contradiction, but when it came to talking about the mystery story, Fred could even muster up a sense of humor.

"This one looks good, but somewhere it just gave up the ghost."

"This one looks like it was written by a committee."

And finally,

"This one shows how a truly successful story ends in a burst of excitement."

For this one he had drawn mostly ascending lines with short horizontal lines and then a last upward stroke, ending with what looked like shooting stars.

It was truly an unusual presentation, something that had never been done before. Everyone watched in rapt attention. At the end of the evening, people urged Fred to write this explanation in book form for students and writers alike. He promised he would but never got around to it.

Somewhere I have his original pencil outlines. He had told me to throw them away but I couldn't part with them. They conjured up such a wonderful memory for me.

I remember the questions he was asked after his presentation. Students wanted to know not only more about the short story but also how to submit their stories. Did they need an agent? The answer was No. Did *Ellery Queen's Mystery Magazine* have any taboos? The answer was yes. Fred would never accept a story in which a child was killed. I found that very poignant.

Fred noted that the magazine's readers were two-thirds women and one-third men. Many readers were school teachers, heads of families and ministers, and most of them had old-fashioned ideas about four-letter words and explicit sexual references. It was, he said, a family magazine that was usually read by at least two and sometimes three generations. First it would be read by the mother and father, then it would be passed on to their children and/or their parents for a read-through. So, he explained, the stories had to be not only of high quality in terms of their writing but also in good taste.

Of course there are always exceptions, like the time in 1950 that Fred published a story by Philip MacDonald called "Love Lies Bleeding" which was about homosexuality. Before that there was a story called "Corollary," set in the black ghetto of Newark, New Jersey and with a black detective as protagonist. It was written by Hughes Allison, a black author who had sent it to the magazine with a cover letter saying that he felt sure Fred would never print it. But it was so well-written that Fred couldn't help but buy it, though he worried that he would receive letters of protest, just as he did a few years later when he reprinted "Judge Lynch," a story of a lynching in the South that had been written by Pulitzer Prize winner T.S. Stribling. That story brought dozens of subscription cancellations from Southern readers.

He once made this profound observation: "People do not realize, and editors should not realize, for it would give them swelled heads, that an editor really plays God throughout his life. He rejects or he accepts; he makes a career or he breaks a career; and it is a very uncomfortable feeling. Only sometimes, if an editor has had a few drinks, he might feel good about himself. How many people can play God? It's a very frightening situation."

Question: "What would happen if a story needed editing?"

Answer: "If I can do a reasonable editing without hurting the story or the writer's feelings, that's fine. If not, but the story has a good theme, I will send it back to the author with a good critique and my ideas on how to change it. A story has to be one in which I believe what the people do. It has to be a unified story in a credible sense. I must believe in the characterization and know that the writer has gotten into the skin of the character. If I can turn page after page and am sorry when the story has ended, that's a winner."

Question: "How can I do that?"

Answer: "The answer is in the following story: A tourist approaches a New Yorker and asks 'How do I get to Carnegie Hall?' And the New Yorker replies, 'Practice, practice, practice!'"

Question: "How long does it take to get a story into print once it's accepted?"

Answer: "At least six months, but usually longer. The only story for which I made an exception was one that came to me from Pete Hamill, the well-known New York columnist. I had never received a story from him and never knew that he wrote mystery stories. I insisted that the story be printed immediately. Not only was it a delightful story, but Pete Hamill was dating Jackie Onassis at the time, so it was truly a 'hot' item."

Question: "Are some stories bought but never published?"

Answer: "As far as I can remember, there were probably no more than three such stories. I do remember one case. Before Dashiell Hammett became famous, he was published in pulps and remained quite unknown. I was lucky enough to find all of these short stories and fortunate enough to offer Hammett an acceptable contract to publish them. Hammett became a prime contributor to the magazine. However, just as one story came out, that same day Hammett was arrested for alleged Communist activities. Those were the dreadful McCarthy days. As soon as the story was published, hundreds of letters came in saying in essence, 'How much of the money you paid Hammett went into the Communist coffers?' In those days one was guilty by association even though not guilty at all. I still had one more contract with Hammett, and I was in a great dilemma and didn't know what to do. I held up that story and did not publish it. I hated to give up that story and held onto it for a long time, for I knew I would never get another Hammett story. I kept it as long as possible and finally published it. I also have Hammett books from those years. Hammett autographed one of them and wrote, 'Thanks, Fred, you are the one that kept my stories from dying on the vine.'"

The Q/A session went on for over two hours. I was amazed that Fred was strong enough to go on answering so many questions in such great detail, and as the time passed he showed no nervousness at all. He actually seemed to be enjoying it more and more. Finally someone said, "Thank you for coming out of your shell." Then he asked, "Have you enjoyed this as much as we have?"

Fred smiled and said, "I must confess it's been very exciting. It's been a long, long time since I appeared in public." And then he shared an even bigger confession: "The dread of my life was public speaking. It was always the bane of my existence, and early in my career I tried my best to cure that dread. Manny Lee, who as you know was my cousin and my writing partner, and I went on a lecture tour for two years all across the country, but at the end of the two years I was just as bad as at the beginning, and not having cured the dread, I said 'The hell with that' and stopped appearing in public."

And then, "So what made you agree to this?"

Fred answered: "My wife, Rose, assured me that I would be just fine with her at my side. So I accepted, and you see, she was right."

And it only got better.

Our First Trip to Japan

A wonderfully exciting surprise had come our way. We had been invited to Japan as guests of Fred's Japanese publishers. Fred had edited and written an introduction for *The Japanese Golden Dozen*, a book of mystery stories by 12 Japanese authors.

Mr. Kozo Igarashi, the head of a large Japanese publishing firm, had written to ask if we would consider coming to Japan concurrent with the publication of the book. He had done everything in his power to get Fred to agree, offering first-class air and several intriguing side trips to Hakone, Mount Fuji, Kyoto, Nara and Hong Kong. Fred did everything in his power to get out of going. He even declined to write to them personally, but rather had me write to them on his behalf.

"Tell them that I'm a diabetic and would need a special diet," Fred told me.

And Mr. Igarashi responded that we needed only to tell him what that diet consisted of, and he would make sure that it was faithfully followed.

"Tell them that I might need a doctor," Fred told me.

And Mr. Igarashi responded that he would make sure that the best English-speaking doctor would be on call for Fred on a 24-hour basis.

At the same time I was assuring Fred that nothing would hurt him as long as he had me beside him. In the short time that we had been married, he had told me several times how much courage I had given him to do so many things that he could never have done before. What a wonderful feeling for me to know that someone I loved trusted me so implicitly!

And then, as we were still debating the merits of the trip, the next letter arrived from Mr. Igarashi. "We are so happy that you are coming to Japan," it read.

Huh? Fred and I looked at each other and wondered out loud just when we had accepted. Our conclusion was that this Japanese gentleman was really clever. And just as I was wondering how I was going to respond, Fred suddenly said, "Okay, we'll go."

I could hardly believe my ears. What in the world had made this reclusive husband of mine, always so averse to travel, decide to go? Was it the cleverness of Mr. Igarashi? Was it his personal doctor who, visiting us socially one evening, had reassured him about his health? Was it a good friend of his, a psychiatrist, who had told him, "Fred, you have to be crazy not to accept a trip like this. Shall I have you committed?" It might have been my son, who had said to him when he had voiced his concern about how much luggage he would have to take with him, "I'll carry your luggage for you, and don't worry, you don't even need to buy a ticket for me. For a trip like this I'll just cling to the tail of the plane with your luggage strapped to my back." Or was it that he knew how much I wanted to go?

The gods were on my side, I suppose, and Fred's side too, for this was to be a most exciting and memorable trip for both of us, a dream come true for me and an ego trip for Fred such as he had never dreamed of. The absolutely unexpected adoration, adulation and hero worship that greeted him in Japan was entirely beyond what he imagined or expected. It was a fitting reward for him. His books had given so much pleasure to so many people all over the world. Never before had he received such an open display of love and admiration from his public.

Still, the morning we were to leave, Fred woke up sounding like a man condemned to death. "Well, this is the day," he said, as he turned on the television to watch the morning news. "If you're lucky, they'll make an announcement that Tokyo has been stolen," I told him. But instead of bringing a smile to his face, he replied, quite seriously, "I wouldn't mind one bit." I tried not to laugh.

As we stepped out of the car at the airport, two young JAL

officials appeared, took our hand luggage, and escorted us to a private lounge. They ordered tea for me, orange juice for Fred and, fearing that the plane meal might be served too late for Fred's lunch, they brought him a sandwich. We were told to relax because we wouldn't be boarding the plane until everyone else had boarded. Once onboard, the flight attendant brought us kimonos, slippers, blankets and hot finger towels. This was the first time we had traveled first class, and I savored the luxury of it. Even Fred seemed to be quietly thrilled by it, and kept squeezing my hand lovingly. Or was it out of fear? I didn't ask. Fred declined the offer of champagne but I accepted, even though it was just around noon and I was not used to drinking so early. It made me immediately euphoric.

We arrived in Tokyo earlier than scheduled, and as we prepared to leave the plane we were surprised to see that all the passengers were being held back until we deplaned. As we descended the stairs, we realized why. To our utter surprise, there were several photographers poised to take photographs of us. A JAL representative introduced himself, then rushed us through customs and landing formalities. Then he escorted us to the airport's main lounge. If we were surprised by the photographers when we deplaned, that was nothing compared to what greeted us in the lounge. We truly had to stop and take deep breaths. There were crowds being held back behind ropes. At least a dozen more photographers were shooting our arrival. Two lovely young Japanese girls approached us with huge bouquets of red roses.

Our Japanese hosts and officers of their publishing houses were bowing, smiling, bowing again, and we did the same. Later we learned that our arrival was being shown on live television. Meanwhile several young people, carrying copies of Fred's books, had broken through the lines and begged Fred for his autograph. He signed a few, and then we were hustled away, escorted through the crowds to a waiting limousine. We were driven to the Tokyo Hilton, accompanied by Mr. Igarashi, who insisted that we call him Kozo, and Mayumi, our interpreter, who acknowledged that we needed a few minutes in our room to freshen up but asked if we would come back down to a press room for a short conference with a few reporters who had been waiting for us at the hotel. Fred felt obliged to say yes, even though we had both figured out that it was about 4 a.m. Larchmont time, and we had gotten very little sleep on the plane. How were we staying awake? It was all the excitement, of course.

Our room turned out to be a suite with sitting room, bedroom, two bathrooms, and a kitchenette with a fully stocked refrigerator. Oh, did I mention the fully stocked bar? On a low table in front of the sofa was a huge platter of fruits and cheeses with a "Welcome Ellery Queen" sign. We were no longer Mr. and Mrs. Dannay. We were Mr. and Mrs. Queen. And like Queens, we were royalty to the Japanese. Alone in our room, we stared at each other in disbelief. Was this really happening to us, this amazing arrival and welcome? Or were we dreaming? We had no idea that this was just the beginning of many days and nights filled with more adventures and even more excitement.

As we entered the press room, photographers' bulbs flashed and excited voices shouted, in English, "He's here!" I counted at least thirty reporters and photographers. "Please hold your flowers this way," one of the photographers said. (We had been presented with two more lavish bouquets.) "Please face this way," another told us. "Now sit and look at each other." All of this was said in Japanese, interpreted by Mayumi. Fred looked bewildered but happy.

Then it was time for the questions. The short conference lasted more than two hours. I sat there in silent admiration, listening to Fred's intelligent answers. Just once was a question directed at me: "What do you look forward to enjoying in Japan?" I can't remember what I answered, but it must have pleased the crowd because they applauded. It was finally over, and we envisioned getting into our beds, but it wasn't that time yet. Kozo announced that we would be meeting someone in the hotel restaurant, a journalist who had arranged for a personal interview and had brought her own photographer. Miraculously, Fred got through the interview, although several times, in his tired state, he would turn to me to ask if his answer was correct. Back in Larchmont we would receive the fruits of Fred's labor, a copy of a prestigious magazine with a long article replete with photographs of Fred and me. When this last interview ended, I said to Fred, "Watch out, dear. We might find a reporter in our bed."

The next morning we embarked on an overnight trip to Mount Fuji and Hakone. A bus was waiting for us and we assumed the letters across the top of the bus indicated our destination. But we were wrong. It said "Ellery Queen." The bus held twenty passengers, all of whom would be traveling with us. Kozo arrived with copies of newspapers so that we could see all of the stories and photographs of our arrival.

The bus was carpeted and, as we entered, we took off our shoes and were given slippers. It was putting our shoes back on that was a new and precarious form of exercise for us. To leave the bus we held onto the railing, slipped out of one slipper, bent over to reach for one shoe, put it on while balancing on the other foot, and stepped down to the first step. We then repeated this same process with the other foot, which was somewhere to the rear, and then stepped down off the bus, hopefully with both shoes on. I was wearing sandals, and often the straps refused to cooperate. Fred wore laced shoes and someone always insisted on tying them for him. Watching us learn this shoe ballet must have been quite a sight, an unusual and ungainly bit of choreography. But we laughed about it and our fellow passengers did too. We chose not to think about whether they were laughing with us or at us.

We quickly learned the art of communicating through our interpreter and were soon asking questions, telling stories, even joking with one another. As a woman I was breaking Japanese customs by talking and joking with these very formal businessmen, but they didn't seem to mind and were wonderfully warm and friendly toward me. At one point Fred said to me, "Your warmth and friendliness, and especially your humor, transcends all cultures." It was a lovely compliment coming from one very tired husband.

As the bus headed into the mountains, a mist hung over the tops of everything like a sheer veil. Mr. Obokata, one of our hosts, noted, "Mount Fuji may be hiding behind her curtain, too shy to come out and face such a famous man as Ellery Queen." Then he added, "It is often impossible to see the top of Mount Fuji, but should you be lucky enough to see it, it will mean that you will see Japan again."

That night, at the Hakone Hotel, there was a party in our honor. We had a private dining room where a huge table was set with a pink starched linen tablecloth, a centerpiece of pink roses, and lighted candles glowing against the dark brown wood paneling of the room. Through the windows we could see the dark night illuminated by a full moon and sparkling lights from the shore reflected in the river. What a perfect night for a party! We were toasted with champagne and everyone was in a festive mood. Just before dessert we were presented with gifts, as though the trip itself wasn't enough of a gift.

The next day we were ferried across the river to the other side of town. We stopped at a shrine in a deeply wooded area, peaceful and almost spiritual in its beauty. The tall old trees were covered with moss. Winding stone paths and flowering shrubs were everywhere. There was a pond stocked with koi. One of our hosts had brought fortune cookies and we were told to break them open, tie the paper slips to a branch of a tree and make a wish. Kozo assured us that doing so would bring us back for another visit to Japan. I'll do anything that will bring us back, I thought to myself. Fortunately, no one told me to jump into the fish pond!

We arrived back in Tokyo early that afternoon but not before we drove past Mount Fuji again. This time we saw the peak in all its white and silver magnificence against a blue sky. And Mr. Obokata was right. We did see Japan again, two years later.

The press and photographers were awaiting our arrival. It seemed that everyone was aware of our every move, including the appointment we were about to have with Mr. Tanabe, the owner of Kinokuniya, one of the world's largest bookstores. As the photographers ran ahead of us to take our pictures, we had to force our way through the store. Fred was quickly recognized, and such a dense crowd formed around us that a security guard was called to make way for us to get to Mr. Tanabe's offices on the top floors of the building.

Mr. Tanabe and Fred became instant friends when they discovered that they were both born in the same month and year, October 1905, and were the only two men present wearing bow ties. Mr. Tanabe presented us with a beautifully illustrated book and an authentic tea ceremony bowl. Before we left his office, he remarked, "I've seen pictures of both of you, and you are always holding hands. I'm so jealous." Then, he reached over, took my hand, and asked his personal photographer to take our picture, without Fred. Everyone was amused and chided him for being such a ladies' man, a reputation that preceded me. From his office he took us to his club to show us a true ritualistic tea ceremony.

At eight a.m. the next morning Fred was scheduled for a live broadcast at a local television station. He was a nervous wreck. This was his first live appearance, and if that wasn't enough, he was worried about the difficulty of the interpretation with a different interpreter. Also I would not be sitting by his side as he had gotten used to. The program was being taped before a live audience to be shown the following morning. It was a show, Kozo told us, that was watched by 20 million people. Our hosts were excited that their families would get to see their Mr. Queen on TV, and Fred would be able to see himself as he ate his breakfast.

As usual, Fred's concerns were for naught. He did himself proud, answering all the questions carefully and without hesitation. I was permitted to watch him on the monitors, and I noticed how handsome he looked. When it was over, I told him that I could see a future career for him as an actor or TV personality. I could tell that pleased him, but not nearly as much as when the anchor man told him that he could hardly believe that this had been Fred's first TV interview.

Back at the hotel there were three more newspaper interviews. The first proved to be the most amusing. It was conducted by a young woman from the Associated Press who was so excited and nervous about meeting Fred that she squirmed and giggled and wiggled with every question. Each time she laughed, I couldn't help but laugh too. Watching us both giggle made Fred hardly able to answer her questions seriously, but he seemed to meet her requirements because, thanking and bowing as she exited backwards, she almost fell over the doorstep. As the door closed, Fred and I looked at each other and laughed some more. It was really sympathetic laughter.

After two more interviews, Fred returned to our suite for a well-deserved rest. I went to the hotel's beauty salon to have my hair done in anticipation of the official welcoming party that night. We hoped it would be a small intimate reception. At 6:30 p.m. several executives arrived at our suite with two huge white chrysanthemum corsages, their stems wrapped in white satin ribbon with long streamers. These were pinned shoulder-high on our clothes. Suddenly we got the sense that this was not a small intimate reception.

As we stepped off the elevator at a floor marked Banquet Room we were greeted by loud applause. Huge "Welcome Mr. and Mrs. Ellery Queen" banners were hung on two walls. But what impressed us most were the two long lines of people forming an aisle that we were to walk through. This was a huge ballroom filled with several hundred people who smiled and bowed as, hand-in-hand, Fred and I walked past them.

We were led to a platform and seated in front of a low black table with roses, tulips and anemones as a centerpiece. It was if we were there to hold court. Guests pressed forward to meet us. We tried to repeat their names as they were formally introduced. Not an easy task, and we feared that many a smile was not in greeting but in polite mirth over our mispronunciations.

The Master of Ceremonies, a professor from Tokyo University who spoke English, welcomed us and praised Fred for the remarkable contribution he had made to the reading pleasure of people throughout the world and especially in Japan. Afterwards one of our hosts spoke in Japanese. Our translators—Fred and I each had one, sitting next to us—repeated what he said in English. It couldn't have been more gracious or flattering.

It was now Fred's turn to speak, and much to my surprise he took my hand and led me to the podium. This seemed to amuse the guests; the Japanese simply didn't hold hands in public. Fred held my hand as he addressed the group, thanking our hosts for their hospitality, acknowledging the wonderful time we were having, and gratefully anticipating all that remained. He looked perfectly at ease and his voice was remarkably strong. He was charming, and everyone responded enthusiastically. I suppose they thought that as long as I was up at the podium, they should ask me to say a few words too, though I wonder whether they figured I would decline. However, I was so overwhelmed by their graciousness, I just couldn't refuse. Fred squeezed my hand and said, "Go ahead, dear. Say something."

Despite my extreme nervousness I managed to express my personal gratitude. I concluded with: "The beauty of Japan is only exceeded by the beauty of its people." How in the world did I ever think that up? I was astonished by the applause but especially by a young woman who rushed up to me and, with tears in her eyes, kissed my hand and exclaimed in English that she had never heard anyone speak so lovingly of her people. I felt like a rock star.

As we headed back to our seats, Fred whispered to me, "Watch out. You'll be getting the rave notices in the press tomorrow!"

The food had been brought to the table, and it looked wonderful.

We were hungry too. But just as we'd pick up our forks to sample the meal, one more person would be brought up to us to be introduced. Before we knew it, the entertainment started, a Japanese welcome dance executed in high spirits by two people in colorful dragon costumes, their huge mouths opening and closing perilously close to us and our food. We felt it would be rude and potentially dangerous to try to keep eating. But when the dance was over, our hosts informed us that it was time to leave. No one else could leave the party unless we left first. With a last look at our dinner we left the banquet room to loud applause. Luckily, when we returned to our suite we found trays of assorted cold meats, fruits and cheeses. And finally we were alone and able to talk about what we had just experienced.

Fred put his arms around me and said, "If it weren't for you, darling, this never would be happening to me."

"If it weren't for you, this never would be happening to me either," I told him.

We were both right. And at that moment I couldn't imagine two people, at any age, anywhere, happier or more in love than the two of us.

The following morning we watched Fred's previous day's broadcast, and loved every minute of it, as we ate a sumptuous breakfast. Then it was off for a two-night stay in Kyoto. Accompanied by several of our hosts as well as by Shizuko Natsuki, Kozo's beautiful and charming sister, who is also a famous author in Japan, which was unusual for a Japanese woman at the time, we were driven to the train station to board the Bullet Train and a special car reserved just for us. A speedometer at the end of the car amazed us when the dial reached 200 miles per hour.

Leaving the train, we were met by two limousines that took us to the Heian Shrine, an exquisite area of wondrous gardens and buildings, of the Chinese influence, painted in vermilion and green. The gates at the entrance were an impressive 70 feet tall. Our tour also included the Golden Pavilion and Silver Pavilion, both framed by tall trees and elegant gardens, all reflected in surrounding ponds. Some walls were completely covered in gold leaf. Inside stood the handsome statues of Buddhist gods. Our last stop was the Imperial Palace, the traditional seat of the Emperor and used for the coronation ceremony. Set high on a hill with large garden pools, the site was designed to give the visitor a superb view from any direction. I was awestruck. "This is truly the quintessence of Japanese beauty," I whispered to Fred.

That night we stayed at Sumiya, a traditional Japanese inn. The owner, his wife and the entire staff were waiting outside for us as our cars pulled up. With words of welcome and much bowing, we were given clogs to get over the stones of the courtyard to the front door, and then soft slippers to walk into the carpeted foyer, and yet another pair as we entered our own room.

The large living room was, as might be expected, furnished in Japanese style: a low table in the center of the room with cushions and backrests around it. The room overlooked a minuscule Japanese garden with the customary stone lantern, small rock-strewn paths, miniature bonsai trees and a tiny fountain. What a wonderful sight! And refreshing, too. Fred and I were so accustomed to Western clutter that we were intrigued by the quiet elegance of these surroundings. It was the perfect setting for afternoon tea. There we were sitting comfortably albeit awkwardly.

Fred said, "We'll have to drink our afternoon tea at home this way." That was said 20 minutes before the leg cramps set in. But before that there was another new adventure awaiting us: Bathing in a Japanese bathroom. Off the foyer and just outside our room was a private bath with red slippers at the door, not to be confused with other slippers that were to be used for the bathroom only. You see, there were two separate rooms. One with the toilet and a small washbasin, the other with a toilet, a wooden-covered hot tub, a low stool which we assumed was to sit on while soaping our feet, and a pitcher of water which, we again assumed, was to rinse off the soap. But when were we supposed to use the water in the tub? And was it to be one at a time or together? The hand-held shower in one corner of the room elicited more questions. It was clear that we needed each other at that moment, so we soaped ourselves up, then tossed water at each other from the large pitcher, trying to control our laughter. What would our hosts think? We sounded like two kids frolicking at the beach. We finished the way we knew best by rinsing ourselves off with the hand-held shower. We then entered the hot tub together, as is the custom. What fun!

Our dinner plans involved a party hosted by ShizukoNatsuki at the Kyo-Yamoto, a traditional Japanese restaurant, high on a hill overlooking the lights of the city below.

As we approached the entrance to the restaurant, one of the geisha girls invited to the party was just arriving, and Shizuko asked if she would pose for a picture with Fred. She was slim, very tall, and gorgeous; she said that she would be honored and the photographer posed the two of them. Fred looked like the cat who swallowed the canary. Luckily, I'm not the jealous type, not even at the dinner table when she sat on her knees between Fred and me, removing covers and handing us each new utensils as we needed them, and anticipating our every need. Well, I'm not exactly sure what Fred's needs might have been, and I didn't ask.

Kozo and Miki came back to the inn with us and informed us there was another room that had been reserved for us. Always thinking of our comfort, this second room had a Western-style bed, just in case we couldn't sleep on the floor on the tatami mats. But we insisted that we at least wanted to try. We slipped into our crisp sleeping kimonos, which were so well-starched they could have stood up by themselves, and lowered ourselves rather gingerly onto our mats and turned off the small lantern-type lamp beside us. As tired as we were, we couldn't fall asleep. We kissed and caressed each other, and before too long we were discovering what lovemaking on a tatami mat was like. As satisfying as anywhere else in the world!

The next day we visited a kimono factory and museum, owned by two of the guests who had attended the dinner party the night before. We were treated to a fashion show of kimonos, and I admired every one of them while Fred admired the beautiful models. It turned out that the kimonos cost upward of $3,000 each, but the owner assured me that if I wished to buy one, it would only cost $1,500. I had only to see the expression on Fred's face to know I had to politely decline. Later Kozo would explain to me that Japanese ladies of wealth owned many dozens of these kimonos, as each season required different patterns and materials. In fact, he said, his sister owned 75. I had admired the kimono she had worn to the party in Tokyo, and now Kozo told me that she had had it made in honor of her meeting Ellery Queen.

From there we headed for Nara, the site of the Kasuga Shrine and the Todaiji Temple, which housed the 728-year-old Daibutsu (Great Buddha), the world's largest bronze statue of the Enlightened One.

***

Meanwhile back at the inn, the owners were personally preparing a dinner for us and the guests from the previous night's party. According to Kozo, the dinner would consist of very special foods that were not easily available during that particular season. That's how eager they were to please their honored guests. Through our translator we told them how much we enjoyed the meal. This seemed to give the wife enough courage to tell us that her husband was a great Ellery Queen fan. With that she excused herself with much bowing, hurried out of the dining room, and returned within minutes with her husband. Each was carrying a large tray laden with Queen books. "To prove she was telling the truth," our interpreter told us. Fred autographed a few of them, which actually brought tears to their eyes. They asked the interpreter to tell us, "We will treasure these books for all our lives."

We left Kyoto the next day and traveled to the Osaka airport by car so that we could see as much of the countryside as possible before catching a flight back to Tokyo. With a free afternoon in Tokyo, Fred rested at the hotel while Miki and I took advantage of the chauffeured Rolls Royce to take us downtown to shop. It was not hard for me to get used to such luxury. That night Kozo had asked us to have dinner with him and his younger son, Shoichi.

The next day was a busy one for Fred and for me. Fred had three interviews to attend. The first one was with a group of his fans, which turned out to be the 300-member "Sealed Room Club," an organization of Ellery Queen fans that had been formed in college. It consisted of its founding members, more recent graduates, and current students as well.

Fred was surprised to find such a young group of fans, so devoted to his work and so excited by his presence. I continued to be amazed at Fred's self-effacement and modesty in the light of so much adulation, but I realized that it was not only his talent but his sense of humility that made him great, and I told him so.

The second interview was with a tall dark-haired lady of Russian and Swedish descent who spoke and wrote perfect English. She was kind enough to send us a copy of her article, all four pages of it.

The third interview was the most difficult of any Fred had given in Japan. It lasted from 3 p.m. to 5 p.m. with several recordings being made simultaneously and photographers constantly taking photographs. This was a meeting with Mr. Seicho Matsumoto, Japan's leading mystery writer. The two men talked about the dynamics of writing the mystery-detective story, Fred from a Western approach, Mr. Matsumoto from the Eastern perspective. Both men were intense and interesting, illustrating their points on blackboards. Much of what they said was interrupted by applause from an audience that consisted of dignitaries, publishers and special fans. As we left the room, everyone stood up and bowed. They're showing their gratitude, we were told.

But that wasn't all. Mr. Matsumoto was holding a dinner in our honor at, we were told, a very elite and elegant French restaurant called Crescent. The food was the quintessence of French cooking, coupled with the esthetic charm of Japanese service. The dining room was ornately decked out with wood paneling, crystal chandelier, and huge fireplace with logs aglow. The conversation was almost entirely between the host and his guest of honor. They talked about books and writing and it was all very formal. Each seemed to be trying to be more profound than the other. Everyone else sat quietly and listened. I couldn't bear to have this lovely dinner turn into a business meeting so, whenever I could, I tried to interject some humorous remark, a light touch which succeeded, I think, in changing the mood and tone of the evening. Yes, it was daring of me, but I felt that this evening should be more than listening to two famous men talking about mystery writing, especially when most of us had already heard it discussed that afternoon.

My boldness was reinforced by Fred beaming at me and every once in a while saying, "That was funny. Keep up the good work."

It was just about time for dessert when Mr. Matsumoto had a tremendous wooden crate brought to our table and unpacked while we watched in great anticipation. It was a present for us, a magnificent handmade figure of a Japanese lady, doll-size and dressed in a traditional kimono enclosed in a glass box. We were surprised by this lavish gift. I assured Mr. Matsumoto it would look wonderful in our living room in Larchmont, and he assured us that we wouldn't have to carry it there.

In truth we were overwhelmed. "How do we thank him?" Fred asked me. Could we really go on accepting gift after gift? Were we giving enough in return just by our presence? Still, I noticed that these generous people seemed happiest when they saw our faces reflect wonder and delight at these unexpected tributes. I also thought that perhaps I should try one more humorous remark.

"Is it true," I said to our hosts, "as I have heard, that our plane back to the United States will be one large 747 with only the crew, Mr. Queen, me, and our gifts?"

The interpreter translated what I had said, and the gentlemen lost all reserve, laughed loudly and applauded. It was evidently the perfect "thank you."

After dinner the owner, a Frenchman, invited us to his private quarters. We walked up a circular staircase and through an electronically controlled red door into a dazzling scene. Several specially designed rooms were lined with floor-to-ceiling glass cases, filled with priceless antiques. Huge pull-out drawers held smaller antique *objets d'art*. Besides being a restaurateur, this gentleman was a famous collector of rare antiquities. We left in awe, feeling that only experts could truly understand this brilliant, quiet-spoken man's remarkable and dazzling treasures.

The next day, after an early breakfast, we were driven to the Tokyo International Airport for a plane to Hong Kong. This was yet another extra given to us for our having accepted the publishers' invitation to Japan. As though being with these wonderful people in Japan wasn't enough!

At the Tokyo airport all JAL personnel were at our side, carrying our bags and coats as they escorted us to the plane. Our party consisted of Mr. Matsumoto, Kozo, an interpreter and two photographers, but none would board until Fred and I went first.

I had a silly thought and said to Fred, "What do you think would happen if we refused to board first?"

And with a most uncharacteristic devilish grin on his face, Fred said, "Let's try it." Of course we didn't.

Rooms had been reserved for us at the Peninsula Hotel, located in an elegant old colonial building fronting the harbor and a symbol of luxury for half a century. The magnificent lobby boasted massive columns and high carved ceilings, with reliefs of mythical figures etched in gold. What an impressive statement it made! Besides being the perfect overnight accommodation, it was *the* place in Hong Kong for visitors to have drinks, light meals and leisurely afternoon teas. It was the place to be seen, and to see the internationally wealthy and famous.

Our rooms faced the harbor with its dramatic view of the skyline and Victoria Peak magically reflected in the waters. After a short rest we were taken to the residence of a millionaire high up in the hills. Mr. Matsumoto was contemplating the plot for a new book and he wanted to see first-hand the contrast between the lives of the very wealthy and the abject poor in Hong Kong.

The house resembled a stage setting. Compared to the simple lines of Japanese architecture, this house had several levels of living space and elaborately carved decorations. The rooms were painted in many bright colors. At the back of the house was a huge mausoleum where, we learned, the owner's grandfather was interred, and where most of the family would eventually be. Astounding!

Our next stop was a famous Chinese restaurant where a dinner was given in honor of Mr. Matsumoto and Fred. The Japanese consul in Hong Kong and several other dignitaries joined us. We were told that the Chinese take pleasure in eating with many friends jammed together under bright lights, noisily enjoying themselves, which was so different from what we had experienced in Japan.

Huge amounts of food were passed around in enormous tureens. Kozo sat between Fred and me to make sure we knew what we were eating. Much was unfamiliar so Fred declined with his customary, "It's not on my diet." There were several times that I wished I had his excuse but I tried everything, even the huge sea slugs.

The next day was set aside for visiting the sights, first a ferry trip from Kowloon to Hong Kong Island, then sightseeing along the narrow streets through Aberdeen, Repulse Bay, and part of the Victoria Peak. We had a noisy, frenetic and fun lunch at a floating restaurant called Jumbo, followed by a trip along the narrow waterway in a sampan. It was unbelievable to see the hundreds of families living on these sampans, most of them no larger than a small room. Boats side by side, with garbage and refuse simply tossed overboard. Despite the floating garbage, children jumped into the water and swam around happily. To me the poverty was abysmal, the stench dreadful. And yet from all outward appearances these boat people seemed quite accepting of their mode of living.

And if I thought this was poverty, there was more of Mr. Matsumoto's book research to come. A visit to the Kowloon Walled City, facetiously referred to as Kowloon Castle. All of our valuables, even our passports, had to be left in our hotel room. We couldn't take anything with us that would attract attention. We walked through several narrow and crowded streets, then we descended a few steps as if to a basement store. Once inside a darkened hallway we walked up a few steps to a narrow pathway paved with cobblestones, dimly lit, with narrow gullies along each side from which emanated a variety of highly unpleasant odors.

We were cautioned to walk single file and as quickly as possible; not to stop, not to talk to anyone, and the photographer accompanying us was ordered not to take photos. Carved out of rock on each side of this tunnel were single rooms with unpainted walls and bare floors, each sparsely furnished with a bed and chair or two. Single electric bulbs hung from each ceiling. As we hurried along, looking from side to side, we were startled to see men lying on floors evidently smoking opium, others sitting in groups gambling. In some rooms women were working on old sewing machines, and boys in undershirts were playing something called *pai lan*, which we were later told was similar to baccarat. In one room a partially clad young woman lay on a bed with a man also half undressed. In another room close by, a young boy was lying on the floor, peering intently into a book under the poor light of the single electric bulb. How moving that was. Even under these adverse conditions, someone was searching for knowledge. My heart was pounding from the emotional and physical experience.

When we finally reached the end of the tunnel and walked up the stairs to the street, we stood gasping for a breath of fresh air. Kozo told us we had actually walked across town.

Though we had hoped to return to our hotel after this strenuous walk, Mr. Matsumoto asked us to accompany him to a Chinese settlement where indigent people had, as the result of a landslide some years previous, been placed in hastily built tin shacks. When they were settled into these temporary shelters, they were promised low-cost apartment housing, but most of them had already been in the settlement for several years with no end in sight. And yet, despite their poverty and helplessness, they were a proud people.

Finally we returned to our hotel. What a contrast to the world of poverty we had just seen!

That afternoon we left Hong Kong for Tokyo. Our flight went smoothly with just some turbulence. What we didn't know until later was that we had been flying just ahead of a typhoon, and our hosts, who remained in Japan, had been very worried about us. They had been calling the airport all afternoon and were relieved to hear that our plane had landed safely. We were glad not to have known this while we were flying.

When we returned to Tokyo we were still in a whirlwind of activity, including a visit to the Tokyo Tower. It was exhilarating but frightening to be up so high, looking down through open metal grids to the many floors below. After dinner that evening we were off to see a play. Without Kozo sitting between Fred and me, explaining the details of the story, we would never have understood it.

The next day, while Fred met with Shizuko, who had asked him for his advice about a new book she was writing, I went shopping with Miki. So we each got to do what we liked best. Fred talking about books, I shopping for clothes. The plan for dinner was that we would savor sukiyaki specialties. What a treat!

Our last night had arrived, and as guests met at our suite before going to an elegant and flawless dinner at the Ogawa-ken, another famous French restaurant, we all looked and felt truly sad at the thought of leaving each other.

As we ate, our hosts made speeches of thanks for our having come to Japan. Fred and I in turn thanked them not only for inviting us to Japan but for the wonderful accommodations and dinners and receptions and side trips they had provided. Of course there were more gifts, shown to us before being packed for shipping to Larchmont. We had never met such generous and loving people. It was absolutely overwhelming.

Mr. Kubota, one of the gentlemen we met, had been hospitalized and was in traction for his back. Believing that he would never forgive himself if he didn't personally say goodbye to us, he actually discharged himself for the evening against his doctor's advice. I had never seen such selflessness, but I realized it was yet another aspect of fine quality of character.

Dinner was over. It was almost time to leave. As Fred and I stood there, I glanced around the room and couldn't believe what I saw. There were our hosts, all with handkerchiefs to their eyes, wiping away tears. Fred and I looked at each other in astonishment. Stoic Japanese? We would never forget their warmth and love.

Shizuko, who had to make the last train to her home in the suburbs, took leave of us first. She and I clung to each other, and we both burst into tears. Then, with about seven of our hosts filling two limousines, we headed for the airport.

Our hosts escorted us to the plane, coming with us as close to the gate as allowed. I threw my arms around each one and hugged them goodbye, even one of the older, more reserved gentlemen, who felt so limp I was afraid he was about to faint in my arms at this public display of affection. Luckily he recovered and, with a big smile on his face and a twinkle in his eyes, hugged me back, quite tightly. I had the feeling that he probably thought this American custom really isn't so bad after all!

Until Fred and I finally and oh how sadly disappeared through the last gate, we all kept waving and throwing kisses to each other as if we were family. We knew we were taking home with us enough extraordinary memories to cherish for the rest of our lives.

The Dick Cavett Shows

On May 23, 1978, Fred was invited to be on *The Dick Cavett Show*.

"That's a wonderful compliment, Fred," I told him. "But on second thought, your eminent reputation in the mystery field deserves such an honor."

He disagreed. "Darling," he said to me, "you don't take such things for granted. There are world-famous men who never get the opportunity to show their genius or artistry. I'm sure I'll flub my lines and feel ridiculous!"

How much of Fred's character those two remarks revealed!

The day for his appearance on the show arrived and, as might be expected, he was in absolute terror. I sympathized but didn't let on. Instead I remained supportive but firm. It's what worked best when he was overcome with worry.

"Just remember that this is the way you are," I would tell him before an important event, "and also remember how it always turns out well in the end."

And he would reply, "Yes, yes, but not this time, I'm sure." It was so predictable. "I'm just as sure that it will be great," I'd reply. And that would end that discussion.

We drove down by limousine to New York City, with Fred's usual change of shirt and flask of orange juice. I held his hand as we sat in the Green Room, waiting for the host to drop in before the show aired and, I hoped, put Fred at ease.

Fred must have gone to the men's room a dozen times, and every time he did I'd pray silently, "Please God. Don't let his zipper break."

When Dick Cavett arrived, he seemed to calm Fred somewhat by saying that once he was on the set, things would fall into place.

"No, dear, he didn't say 'you'll fall on your face'," I jested.

Dick laughed, and Fred seemed less tense as the two men walked to the stage.

Three, two, one. Quiet on the set.

"Please welcome one of the giants of the mystery field, Mr. Frederic Dannay, better known as Ellery Queen," Dick announced to great applause.

And the first words out of Fred's mouth were, "I'd acknowledge the applause but I'm tongue-tied."

But Dick of course was masterful at untying his guests' tongues, and this time was no exception. He asked all the right questions. Here's a sampling:

"Is there any stigma attached to the mystery story, as in the phrase, 'Oh, he's only a mystery story writer'?"

"Yes, there definitely is," Fred replied. "Mystery writers have been second class citizens for a long time, ever since Poe, and most of us work extra hard to raise the level of appreciation. I'm afraid we've only partially succeeded. We still get reviewed in the back columns of the newspaper or magazine, and we're still considered only entertainment instead of literature."

"I think all good writing is entertainment, no matter what it's about," Cavett noted diplomatically.

"It should be," Fred replied. "Novels should all have the characteristics of mystery including suspense and conflict. The detective story is a very difficult form. I consider it an artistic form. Many serious writers have attempted to write mystery stories, usually under an assumed name, and they've failed. They couldn't master the technique."

Of course, Dick asked one of the most-frequently asked questions of Fred. "How did you get started writing?"

To Dick's question about the type of stories he and Manny wrote, Fred replied, "We started in what was then called the Golden Age of detective stories. It's a very difficult form. We were expected to come up with ingenious and difficult plots, an original concept such as a locked room murder, a miracle problem or an impossible crime. All quite subtle and very legitimate. We had to play absolutely fair with the reader in terms of clues, and we were also expected, whenever possible, to end with a stunning surprise. Add all of these elements together and, you see, you don't have an easy technique to work with. We wrote these types of mysteries from 1929 to 1936, but we began to feel that they were rather artificial and immature. So after 1936 we started to write stories which would better adapt to serialization in magazines or films. Then in 1942 we began to think of writing serious novels within the framework of a detective story. This was a tremendous change. More emphasis was placed on deeper ideas, characterizations and background, and serious social issues."

D.C.: "Which would you say were your best stories?"

F.D.: "No question in my mind that the best quality stories we produced were our later novels. We were older, we were more mature, we had deeper ideas. We began to think in terms of larger meanings and concepts. For example, in *The Glass Village* our focus was McCarthyism. In *The King is Dead* it was about Fascism. We wrote a book about gerontology, and only one critic used the word 'gerontology' in his review. I often wondered if the other critics knew what the book was about. When the Dead Sea Scrolls were found, I became very interested in them and read everything I could about them. I was determined to do a book about them in the framework of a modern detective story to show the life as seen in the Scrolls, the life of the Essenes. That book was called *And On the Eighth Day*.

Dick wanted to know about the actors who had played the role of Ellery Queen on radio.

Fred replied: "Playing Ellery Queen was irresistible. Every actor playing that role became so identified with the role that he became the character. Each one would have loved to have been a brilliant private investigator, a hero to at least some people, and they actually started to live as if they were Ellery Queen. In fact I met a doctor, a pediatrician, who told me how he had once been called down to Greenwich Village to treat a sick child and was told the person calling him was Ellery Queen. The doctor, interested in meeting the famous author, went to the address to treat the child. After taking care of the child and meeting the father, he was told to send the bill to Ellery Queen at that address. Needless to say, it turned out to be the actor who was playing that role at that time."

Dick seemed fascinated with Fred's on-stage presence and the stories he told, and asked Fred if he would come back for another interview.

Fred agreed, despite the fact that he had been so nervous about the first one, and when it ended he still seemed in a daze. As he stood receiving congratulations from the show's staff and some of the audience, I walked up to him and said, "Fred, darling, you were absolutely marvelous."

He looked at me blankly, put out his hand to shake mine, and said, "Thank you very much, madam." Then, suddenly recognizing me, he laughed out loud, put his arm around me, and asked, "Did I really do well?"

Despite the second invitation from Dick, despite the applause, and despite all the sincere congratulations he was receiving, he still wondered if he had done well. I couldn't believe it! When would I ever learn?

The second show came just a few weeks after the first broadcast. Fred, though still nervous, seemed just a little more secure about the routine and his ability to handle it. Fred asked to hear the tape recording I had made of the first show, and as he listened to it he kept saying, "Is that really me?"

Dick started the second program by saying, "The brevity of this half-hour show is sometimes frustrating to me, but never more so than when I had Mr. Frederic Dannay on recently. He had such interesting reminiscences and such mystifying puzzles; the obvious solution was to have him back. Please welcome Frederic Dannay again."

In answer to a question about his choice of career, Fred responded, "If I had my choice I don't think I would be a writer at all."

"Now you think of it!" Dick interjected before Fred continued. "If I had my life to live over again, and that's a beautiful thought for a man past 72, my first choice would be to become a psychiatrist. I have a double reason: one, I think I'm a born snoop; and two, I would be terribly interested in the secret lives of people."

And Dick interjected, "I have both those qualifications too. We could become a team."

Fred continued, "If I couldn't be a psychiatrist I would prefer to be an artist, which actually was my first ambition in life. I studied at the Art Students League, and I even earned a living for some time as an art director. I realized early that there was a tremendous gap between a first-rate artist and a second-rate artist. I knew I couldn't be a first-rate artist, and I didn't think I'd be happy being a second-rate artist, so I opted for something else. The third thing I'd like to do, which would surprise my family and friends, would be my desire to be an actor. Mostly I would want to be an actor because I can be many different people in a lifetime. And I still haven't mentioned 'writer'."

D.C.: "So you didn't get to be three out of the four of the things you might have been. That's nice to hear in a way."

F.D.: "Dick, I feel I've been very lucky because I found something to do which not only turned out to be very rewarding but which was great fun. I always wrote with my cousin, Manny Lee, and there is a great sense of dependency, which can be a problem, of course, when you've worked with a partner for almost a lifetime. So I decided to write a book about my boyhood, a novel. This was a therapeutic thing and a substitute for a psychiatrist's couch. I wrote this novel which was called *The Golden Summer*, and when it was written and published, my dependency hang-up vanished, and I have never given it another thought."

D.C.: "But you needed that. You had to break through that barrier."

F.D.: "You have to prove to yourself at least once that you can do it."

Again Dick asked Fred to play his mystery games with him. Fred gave Dick two more puzzles which Dick couldn't solve. Fred gave him the solutions and Dick said laughingly, "I don't want to play with you anymore. You're too smart."

The show ended to much applause.

Fred felt most comfortable at his home in Larchmont,
but with Rose's encouragement he became a traveler.

Welcome to the Montcalm. Old World charm in London. When the hotel management discovered a famous writer in residence, they asked Fred and Rose to re-enact their arrival and registration for a photographer.

A royal welcome to "Mr. and Mrs. Queen." Two visits to Japan "proved an ego trip for Fred such as he had never dreamed of." The Japanese loved the Ellery Queen novels, and publishers and filmmakers pulled out the stops for Fred and "Mrs. Queen."

Fred and Rose flank Japanese publisher Kozo Igarashi.

The couple at an unidentified locale.

In 1978, Fred and Rose visited Israel, where the finding of the Dead Sea Scrolls had inspired the Queen novel *And On the Eighth Day*.

Fred signs at a fundraiser for the Robert F. Kennedy Action Corps in 1981.Rose chats with autograph-seeker Pat Kennedy Lawford as daughter Dale Koppel looks on. Upper left: Marvin Traub, chairman of Bloomingdales.

Fred receives an honorary doctorate from Carroll College in
Wisconsin in April 1979. Asked to deliver a speech, he would be
tongue-tied. But prompted by questions about mystery-writing,
"he could speak without hesitation or fear" and hold an audience
for hours. Asked how he would advise aspiring writers, he repeated
what he had told a creative writing class that afternoon: "You can't
teach writing. But you can help; you can improve; you can
correct; you can encourage; you can even inspire, which
is a very worthwhile thing to do."

And on the Eighth Day, Israel

In September 1978, right after we returned from Fire Island's calm and peaceful togetherness, we started to plan a trip to Israel.

I wish I could remember just how this trip evolved. I always knew that Fred really wanted to visit Israel. We had talked about such a trip many times but we had been warned by friends that it was strenuous. Too strenuous for Fred?

In large part Fred's interest in Israel came from his book *And On the Eighth Day* which, as he explained on *The Dick Cavett Show*, had been inspired by the finding of the Dead Sea Scrolls in Israel. He often talked about Israel as the land of the Bible, its mysteries, its prophets, Christ's birthplace, the valiant fight of the Jewish people for a homeland of their own. He also thought about the possibility that there was much there to inspire a new mystery story.

As always, I was willing to travel with Fred to new places and meet new people. Not just willing but enthusiastic.

Our travel agent worked quickly. She suggested that we leave on October 18th with a group tour which included first-class air and hotels and sightseeing. Fred opted out of the latter, deciding that it would be too strenuous a routine. Instead we ordered a private limousine and driver so we could plan our days and trips at our own convenience. Of course, after Fred decided on a course of activity, small or large, there always followed his period of doubt. This time was no exception.

"Darling," he said, right after our reservations had been confirmed, "I've written out some questions for you to ask our agent. Please double-check on our tickets, the time of leaving, the hotels, and whatever else you think necessary. And oh, yes," he added. "Please be sure to ask if there's any violent involvement now between Lebanon and Israel, and if so, should we cancel our reservations because of danger?"

Wisely, our travel agent suggested that she speak to Fred directly and assure him that things were quiet and peaceful at the time, and that he mustn't hesitate to take the trip.

We arrived in Israel on October 19th and it was for us, as for most people, an emotional and thrilling experience. When we stepped off the plane, we just stood still for a few minutes, holding hands, and looking at each other with expressions that indicated everything we felt. My first thoughts were of the six million Jews who had been killed just for being Jews. Here we were in a new state hopefully to be preserved for the salvation and preservation of a people who had been without a homeland for many generations. I was tearful, and could see in Fred's face that he too was in a reflective mood.

We learned very quickly that there was too much to be seen in 15 days, even with a private car and Avi, our driver. But what we did get to see was fascinating: Jerusalem with its ancient historical places; the Wailing Wall; the Jaffa Gate; the Citadel; the Armenian Quarter; Zion Gate.

Fred had been talking since the start of our visit about his desire to walk the route that Christ had walked. We walked along the 14 Stations of the Cross, starting from the Convent of Flagellation, Via Dolorosa to the Church of the Holy Sepulcher. Avi and I had to help Fred up this hilly narrow passage. Despite the effort, Fred was elated by the experience. When we reached the end of the road and Fred had caught his breath, he said, very quietly, "And to think that Christ carried a heavy wooden cross all along this route!"

The most emotionally draining experience was our visit to Yad Vashem, that sad and touching memorial to the Jews murdered by the Nazis. We walked down an Avenue of the Righteous Gentiles, a tribute to the many Christians who helped save Jewish lives during that dreadful period, into the uncut stone building, the inside lighted by flares which created eerie shadows on the walls. Here we saw the photos and effects of history from the concentration camps. I was completely spent emotionally, in tears and almost unable to walk as we looked at the horrors of that infamous period in history, so vividly portrayed.

Fred was very interested in the Shrine of the Book, a building with an onion-shaped top, designed to resemble the jar covers in which the Dead Sea Scrolls were discovered. The building houses these scrolls and documents of second-century findings at Masada and the Qumran Cave. He studied these exhibits carefully, and I could tell he was having emotional reactions to them because of their connection to his book *And On the Eighth Day*.

When we visited the Al-Aqsa and Dome of the Rock mosques, Fred was nervous about having to leave our shoes outside. He was sure he would not find them again. As a diabetic he was always extremely concerned about injury to his feet, so he was understandably relieved to find the floors inside covered with deep-piled Oriental rugs which were very comfortable to walk on. The interiors were fascinating with their Byzantine art and architecture, the stained glass ceiling and the blue, green and yellow tiles in the geometric design lining the walls. We were so absorbed by the sacred hushed atmosphere of these beautiful interiors and the quiet intensity of the congregants at prayers that we stayed longer than we had expected.

As we exited, Fred paused for a moment, pointed, and then suddenly shouted, "Look, there they are! There they are!" People around us started looking in the same direction, thinking probably they were about to see some famous people. But the only celebrities were Fred's grey suede shoes.

It was around this time that Avi happened to ask Fred rather casually what his profession was. Avi had already told us about himself. He was born in Belgium, went to the university there, was married to an Israeli-born woman, and had two school-age children.

He was very knowledgeable about Israel and its history and very aware of the politics of the world. We had some very interesting discussions with him during our daily trips and luncheons.

Fred in his usual modest way replied, "I'm a writer."

Avi waited for Fred to continue, but when he realized that that was all the information Fred was offering, he then asked, "Do you write in any particular field?"

"Yes," said Fred. "Mysteries."

Another minute or so passed before Avi asked for the next clue. "Do you write under your own name or a pen name?"

"The latter," Fred answered.

At that I just laughed out loud, which must have encouraged Avi to ask, "May I know what your pen name is?"

"Now get out of that one," I said to Fred.

He couldn't.

"My cousin and I wrote under the name of Ellery Queen," he replied.

With that Avi pulled off the road, turned around looking hard at Fred, and shouted, "My God, I've probably read every one of your books! I was an avid fan of yours even in Belgium. Never could I have imagined that I would meet you in my lifetime, Mr. Dannay. And to think I have the honor of driving you around Israel."

I was pleased that my incognito husband had been found out again.

As outwardly shy and modest as he was, there was no doubt that Fred enjoyed this surprise and admiration of a fan so enthusiastic. By the following day Avi had found two Ellery Queen books, published in Hebrew, for Fred to autograph.

One day Avi asked if we would like to visit one of his cousins who was living in a newly formed kibbutz. This would be a first-hand look at the day-to-day life of the young Israeli settlers. We eagerly accepted his offer.

As we drove along, Fred and I noticed that Avi's attention was rooted on the surrounding countryside. I said to Fred in a whisper, "Doesn't Avi seem tense? Do you think this is his first time in this area?"

Fred replied, "I would hardly think so; but you're right, he does seem tense."

Later that day, as Avi slipped out of his seat, he accidentally pulled aside an old blanket which I had noticed always lay at his side. Under the blanket was a rifle. We were shocked. It had never occurred to us that in addition to being our driver he was also our bodyguard. As we rode up the hill he kept on the lookout for possible snipers. It had a chilling effect on us.

Fred's anonymity couldn't last forever. While we had been exploring on our own, Avi had been telling another driver who his passengers were. He in turn had told his passengers, and on our return we found ourselves surrounded by several young people from Canada with paper and pens in hand for Fred's autograph. They kept asking Fred questions about his writing, and though Fred loved to talk about the mystery field, we had another visit on our itinerary that day. We were on our way to Nazareth and one of Christianity's holiest shrines, the Basilica of the Annunciation.

It had truly been a whirlwind trip for the two of us, and we were sorry it was over. At the airport, the usual security check seemed more stringent. For worriers like Fred and me, the thoroughness and attention to details pleased us, and we didn't mind the delay. We were surprised that we were not being boarded at the gate but taken by bus out to the far end of the field. Having found our seats, we were then told there would be a further delay. The crew was awaiting a special passenger.

As we wondered about this, there was a burst of applause as a small party of people entered the plane. We had an excellent view of the door were surprised to find among our fellow passengers Prime Minister Menachem Begin and his wife. We were actually close enough to shake hands with him as he ascended the stairs to the upper part of the 747 plane, which had evidently been reserved to accommodate his party. He was pleasant, smiling and greeted everyone. Mrs. Begin, clutching a huge bouquet of roses, smiled and waved. We marveled that they were flying on a commercial airline. Didn't they have their own private jet like American presidents?

As we took off and I silently said goodbye to Israel, I thought of the words I had seen at the Diaspora Museum: "Remember the Past, Live in the Present, Trust in the Future." We would never forget this trip.

The 50ᵗʰ Birthday Party

In 1929 Fred and Manny had had their first novel published, so it was fitting that an Ellery Queen fiftieth birthday party, celebrating the anniversary of *The Roman Hat Mystery*, was hosted by Carol Brener, owner of the Murder Ink bookstore, on January 26, 1979, at the Lotos Club, a well-known private club in New York City.

At the same time Otto Penzler, owner of the Mysterious Press as well as a mystery fan and columnist for *Ellery Queen's Mystery Magazine*, published a special Golden Anniversary edition of the book, both a regular trade edition and a slipcased limited edition, signed and numbered by Fred.

What a wonderfully festive party this was! Enlisting my help, Carol had consulted with Fred several times and won him over, despite his many typical protests, to be the guest of honor at this celebration. As usual, his only condition was No Speech, but he was amenable to answering questions. Carol decided to send questionnaires to the guests: writers, fans, publishers, friends and family. When she received the questions, she forwarded them to Fred so that he could prepare his answers. She also included a personal note that read, "I will be there throughout the evening, alternately stunned and delighted that Murder Ink is host to the fine and famous Ellery Queen!"

Invitations called for cocktails at 6:30, with dinner to follow at 7:30 in the ballroom, which held 130 people. We filled the room to capacity.

Of course, as he readied himself the night of the event, his fears surfaced, more than usual perhaps because he was to be the guest of honor. In fact, he noted later in his introductory remarks, "I was so nervous when I arrived, I did not recognize my older son when he greeted me." I had tried hard to keep him calm. I laid out his clothes for the evening and, as he was putting on the trousers, the zipper broke. Luckily he had more than one dark suit in his closet, but it certainly unnerved him. Thankfully, he spared the audience the story of the broken zipper.

Carol had organized everything beautifully. The ballroom was decorated in black and white, and each guest received a black mask, a black cardboard gun with the name Ellery Queen on it, and black top hats. Wine was poured from ebony bottles labeled "Ellery Queen, The Roman Hat Mystery Detective Wine," an excellent beverage which for some mysterious reason was never carried by my liquor store.

The evening festivities were presented in menu form:

Murder Ink Presents

ELLERY QUEEN'S 50TH BIRTHDAY PARTY
Guest of Honor: FREDERIC DANNAY

PART ONE
I. In Which Are Introduced An Author, His Family, Friends, And Fans
II. And Cocktails And Hors d'Oeuvres Are Enjoyed In The Library

PART TWO
III. In Which The Assembled Go To The Ballroom
IV. And Toasts Are Proposed

PART THREE
V. In Which The Dinner Begins With Consomme With Cappelletti
VI. In Which The Second Course Is Salad of Mixed Greens, Vinaigrette
VII. In Which The Entrée Is Roast Rack of Veal, Bouquetiere
VIII. In Which Dessert is Profiteroles
IX. And Coffee, Tea, Sanka, And Brandy Are Offered

INTERLUDE
In Which the Mysterious Mr. Penzler Appears and Presents The Guest
of Honor

PART FOUR
X. In Which Mr. Dannay Conducts More Informal Conversation
XI. – And Explains.

Professor, translator and occasional mystery writer Donald Yates, an Ellery Queen devotee since his teens, wrote a poem for the occasion and read it during dinner. He was kind enough to give me the original, which I still treasure.

For Fred Dannay

First things are those that shape us when we're young,
Revealing new designs we duly heed,
Even before our childhood's song is sung,
Directing where our steps are going to lead.
Ellery Queen was one of those first things
Recharging my boy's mind with awesome thoughts
In him I found the joy that reading brings
Consider this: I found life in those plots.

Despite small choices for the young boy's dream
An ever kinder fate made me your friend,
No one begs full praise, so it would seem
Nor seeks the debt such praise might comprehend
And yet, I stand here, wanting something said
You fathered my career, I'm grateful Fred.

Otto Penzler spoke glowingly of Fred, saying he was the most important and famous American mystery writer outside of Edgar Allan Poe. He told of Fred's and Manny's 40 novels, seven books of short stories, and numerous anthologies and bibliographies. He spoke of the intricate plots as "ingenious and complex, yet giving all clues with all fairness to the reader which was a trademark of the Ellery Queen books." He described the "challenge to the reader" just before the end of a book and before the author's divulgence of the real murderer, which Ellery Queen readers loved so much. Otto confessed that for him personally the most frustrating and tantalizing part of a Queen story was the "dying clue."

He called the collaboration of the two cousins the most famous in mystery fiction and "perhaps in all literature." He went on to discuss *Ellery Queen's Mystery Magazine*, which Fred by himself had started and had served as editor these many years; how the magazine and the detective short story might have died had Fred not kept it alive by giving young new writers their first chance to be published; how Fred had discovered and helped along in their careers the most famous mystery short story writers, among them Stanley Ellin, Robert L. Fish and Lillian de la Torre; how *EQMM* had published the work of 16 Nobel laureates and over 30 Pulitzer Prize winners. He said many more wonderful things about Fred's role in the mystery field before asking him to say a few words. As Fred stood up, he was greeted by a standing ovation and sustained applause.

Now it was Fred's turn. He thanked Otto for the introduction and added that he agreed with everything Otto said. Of course that made the audience laugh. Now that was such a droll departure from Fred's usual modesty that I wondered where it came from, how and why. Might I be able to bottle it for the future?

"This is the second greatest ego trip of my professional life," Fred continued. "The first greatest ego trip happened a little over a year ago when my wife Rose and I were invited to Japan by my publishers and were given the most royal treatment. I thought at that time that there is a biblical saying that a prophet is without honor in his own country. And then came tonight, with this great event and great honor for which I am deeply grateful. So I'd like to revise that biblical saying and say that a prophet is *not* without honor in his own country."

He paused to wait for the applause to die down. Then he said, "This is a night of gladness for me but also a night of sadness. Sometimes gladness and sadness come at the same time. The sadness of this night is that Manny Lee is not here to share this honor and pleasure, and I know you will all join me in a special standing toast in a tribute to the memory of my partner for 43 years, Manfred Lee." Everyone stood up in tribute to Manny's memory but also, I believe, to Fred in tribute to this heartwarming gesture.

There were many questions about the Queen books and stages of their writing, the origin of *EQMM*, the cousins' lecture tours, their techniques in writing, comparisons between their early and later books. Everyone sat spellbound by Fred's answers; he was verbal and impressive and stimulating. He was tremendously happy by this show of respect and devotion.

Just as we thought the evening was coming to a close, there was one more surprise. A few amateur lyricists among the writers had written the following song in honor of the birthday party, sung to the tune of the then-popular Mickey Mouse Club theme song:

> Who's the greatest sleuth of all,
> The best among all men?
> E-L-L-E-R-Y Q-U-E-E-N.
> Ellery, Ellery,
> Forever, let us raise our pince-nez high.
> Come along, and sing our song,
> We'll spell it out again
> E-L-L-E-R-Y Q-U-E-E-N.
>
> Who's the greatest sleuth of all,
> The best among all men?
> E-L-L-E-R-Y Q-U-E-E-N
> Fifty years, we shout and cheer,
> Let's raise the glass – Amen!
> ELLERY QUEEN
> ELLERY QUEEN,
> (Drury Lane),
> Ellery Queen
> (Drury Lane)
> Forever let us raise our pince-nez high, high, high, high.
> Come along and sing our song,
> We'll spell it out again—
> E-L-L-E-R-Y Q-U-E-E-N!

Okay, so it was silly and childlike. And we and everyone else loved every minute of it. The evening was a great success. It's not surprising that Fred and I reminisced about it often, and sometimes even found ourselves singing, or at the very least humming, the E-L-L-E-R-Y Q-U-E-E-N song!

The Honorary Doctorate

On April 17, 1979, Fred received an Honorary Doctoral Degree from Carroll College of Waukesha, Wisconsin.

How could this honor happen to a man like Fred who sought no honors and was so desirous of being private and unnoticed? It goes something like this:

John Ball was a professional friend of Fred's, a mystery writer whose first novel, *In the Heat of the Night*, had become a hit movie. Carroll College, John's alma mater, wished, so John told Fred, to honor him. John of course was the moving spirit behind this desire. We would meet John often at the Mystery Writers of America annual dinner, where he told Fred many times that the college wanted to honor him. After each encounter Fred would say to me, "Oh, you know John, he means well but he dreams up things that never come to pass."

Imagine then how surprised we were when, sometime early in 1979, John called and said that the college had set April 17, 1979 as the day.

Fred put down the phone, turned to me, and said, "I don't really believe this. We should definitely not make any plans until we have some confirmation from the school."

Well, it did come. A letter from Carroll College formally requesting our presence arrived in the mail. Later came a telephone call from a pleasant and extremely efficient lady, Mrs. Genevieve Caspari,

Director of Public Relations, giving us all kinds of travel information. It was all very exciting and I wasted no time in calling the airline to make our plane reservations.

At the same time Fred was already saying, "I hope there won't be a snowstorm, and we won't be able to go." Or was he was secretly wishing there would be?

From the moment we arrived in Waukesha, on Monday, April 16th, 1979, and were met by Mrs. Caspari, activity started. John Ball and most of our friends had already arrived. The attendees included Bob Fish, one of whose novels had been the basis for the Steve McQueen movie *Bullitt*; Mike Nevins, law professor and mystery writer and the author of *Royal Bloodline: Ellery Queen, Author and Detective*; Ned Guymon, an old friend of Fred's from California who, like Fred, was a collector of mystery first editions; bibliographer of crime fiction Al Hubin and his wife Marilyn; Randolph Cox, a librarian and long time mystery fan; Don Pendleton, creator of The Executioner, and his wife; and Steve Stilwell, book dealer and mystery fan. All of them had traveled long distances to be with Fred, who was genuinely happy to see them and grateful for their presence.

We had a tour of the Carroll campus and met Dr. Robert V. Cramer, president of the college. Fred was interviewed by two newspapers, the Milwaukee *Sentinel* and the Waukesha *Freeman*. That evening we had dinner with Dr. James Vopat, Associate Professor of English, and friends. Without a doubt we experienced true mid-Western hospitality.

The following morning's schedule included photo sessions and a TV interview. That afternoon Fred lectured to a creative writing class. He so enjoyed talking to young people; he felt that any help he could give them in their future careers was a way to "pay forward" the good fortune of his own career.

After the lecture there was a book signing reception at the library to which the public had been invited. It was a wonderful turn-out.

It was clear to me that Fred was genuinely excited about this honor. Even though he had so keen a mind, was so naturally intelligent and so well-read that he needed no degree to prove his intellectual excellence, he always regretted that he had not had the chance to attend college.

The hour of the convocation came and yes, Fred was nervous. So was I. The auditorium was immense, the audience large, and the occasion important. Fred had said earlier to Dr. Cramer, "I realize that it is incumbent upon a doctoral candidate to make a speech but I honestly cannot do it. I'll be absolutely tongue-tied, and nothing will come out of my mouth."

It was therefore agreed, though it had never been done this way before, that several of the writers present would be seated on the podium and would ask Fred questions. I don't think I could ever figure out how Fred could be too nervous to give a speech in public, but ask him a question in his field and he could speak without hesitation or fear.

Fred gave a short thank-you for the honor bestowed upon him by saying, "Tonight has been so moving that I am speechless or almost speechless. But I do want to take this opportunity to thank everyone who is connected with Carroll College, to thank them for an honor which they do not realize themselves how great it is to me."

What might have been a short speech, had Fred not insisted on an alternative, turned out to be a long, brilliant panel discussion.

Don Pendleton asked, "What is the most difficult fictional case you have had to solve?"

And Fred replied, "It was a book that came out as *Ten Days' Wonder*. I'm going to commit the unpardonable sin of telling you what the concept of that book was, because if you read it, you wouldn't know the concept until the very end.

"*Ten Days' Wonder* is about a criminal who sets out to break every one of the Ten Commandments. Frankly, what would be molded in one cohesive, unified plot took me ten years. Not the whole ten years, but I kept getting into locked chambers, I kept getting into one-way streets and couldn't find myself a way out, and it took ten years to complete *Ten Days' Wonder*."

Bob Fish asked, "When you started your first book, you had no idea how many books you would list in the end. Yet when you started another series, you called the first book *The Tragedy of X*, which obviously meant that you would have *Y* and *Z* after *X*, otherwise you certainly would have called it *The Tragedy of A*. In other words, you started that series apparently knowing you would write only three books in that series. It was a bit strange."

And Fred answered, "The Drury Lane or the Barnaby Ross series was done because at that time my partner Manny and I were entering into full time writing careers, and at that time no publisher was willing to publish more than two books a year with the same author's name. So we introduced two Ellery Queen books a year. But we found that we couldn't support two families on two Queen books a year. We had to find another publisher for another pair of books in that year. So we invented a new character called Drury Lane, a retired Shakespearean actor turned detective. Now we started with X because it lent itself very well to the plot that we had in mind. When we did X, we followed it with Y naturally, and at the end we followed it with Z. And at that time the critics were giving us ideas. One critic said that we could make a fourth book called *The Tragedy of Ampersand*, and another critic said that we were in a perfect position to start with the alphabet all over again and make the next book *The Tragedy of A*, then *The Tragedy of B* and *C*, and so on. Most writers have trouble getting titles, even writers of very serious books. And here we were offered about 26 titles. So, why did we stop at Z? We found out that it took exactly the same length of time to write a Barnaby Ross book as it took to write an Ellery Queen book, and an Ellery Queen book earned much more money. That's why we called the fourth book *Drury Lane's Last Case*. We killed him off."

Don Pendleton asked, "What would you tell today to aspiring writers, what sort of advice would you give them?"

And Fred responded, "It's the same advice I gave to the creative writing class this afternoon. In the first place you can't teach writing. But you can help; you can improve; you can correct; you can encourage; you can even inspire, which is a very worthwhile thing to do. There has to be a spark in that person, a spark that responds to a teacher who encourages and inspires, and that spark will develop into professionalism. But the only rule, the only rule I know, especially for young people, is that they write and they write some more and then they write still more and they keep on writing until they have corrected the errors of beginning writers. They can be encouraged by teachers and inspired by teachers to do more and better work. But work, writing—either word you want to use—is the secret of becoming a successful writer. I don't know any other formula."

To this answer Bob Fish interjected, "I'd like to add one more thing. If you want to be a successful mystery writer, the chances of your being published are a thousand times better if you send your stories to *Ellery Queen's Mystery Magazine*. *Ellery Queen's Mystery Magazine* makes it a point—the only magazine, I might add, in the world, that makes it a point—to look for previously unpublished writers for every single issue. I want to say this is the innovation of Ellery Queen, and Fred Dannay in particular, that got me started in writing, that got Stanley Ellin writing, and many, many other writers. And without that encouragement I know I wouldn't have become a writer."

This was an outstanding moment in Fred's life, this honor bestowed upon him close to his 74th birthday.

Our Second Trip to Japan
(And a Side Trip to Bangkok)

In 1979 we received our second invitation to Japan. This time it was from the film company which had produced the Japanese version of *Calamity Town*, one of Fred's favorite Queen novels. We knew they were making the picture because we had been present at the meeting with the principals of the company on our first trip, and I had taken notes for Fred regarding the terms and conditions agreed upon. The contract had been signed after we had returned to New York and the stated amounts paid. That, we thought, was the end of the transaction.

But here we were with an invitation to be present at the premiere of the film in Tokyo. What a happy development, I thought, especially since as a further enticement we were offered a side trip to Bangkok.

Fred thought about the trip for days while I patiently waited for him to make up his mind. By patiently I mean I kept down my mentioning how great a trip it would be to once or twice a day. Finally Fred asked me to write and accept the invitation. Done! I didn't give him time to change his mind. Still, as I might have expected, every morning, as Fred awoke and realized what he had done, he would say, "I wish I could cancel it."

On the day of departure Fred said, weakly this time, "I can't believe we're on our way to Tokyo again."

I too hardly believed it.

We were traveling first class, so as soon as we were airborne, we were served champagne. Fred declined but I couldn't resist. I felt in a celebratory mood, and the champagne seemed like an appropriate beverage for the occasion.

Just as on our last trip, photographers greeted us upon our arrival. We acted pleasantly surprised, though I think we might have been disappointed had they not been there. We had been spoiled by all the attention last time.

Too bad the photographers didn't follow us to the immigration desk where we had to have our visas validated. They missed an astonishing episode. We had not remembered that we needed visas. It wasn't entirely our own stupidity. On our last trip the visas had been handled by our hosts.

Fred and I were in a state of panic. The authorities informed us in no uncertain terms that we could stay in Japan no longer than 72 hours without visas. We went from one official to another. explaining our oversight, but to no avail.

Desperate, we paged our hosts, who were at the airport. In seconds, three executives and Kozo came dashing to our rescue.

Now it was their turn to plead with the officials. Finally the head of immigration ruled that an appeal would have to be made the next morning to the Minister of Transportation. Still, he insisted that we would have to be confined to the hotel at the airport. It was only after more pleas by Kozo, and after we filled out long triplicate forms and relinquished our passports, that we were released to our hosts and the hotel in town. We were mortified to have had to involve our hosts in this three-hour ordeal.

Two movie starlets presented us with two slightly wilted bouquets of roses. As tired as we were, we were excited that we were back with our Japanese family again, as we greeted old friends and met new ones from the movie company.

The following day we got to view the Japanese film version of *Calamity Town* at the offices of the president of the film company. Both Fred and I had re-read the book before we left home, and with our interpreter quietly telling us what the characters were saying, we thought the movie was very well done, the story carefully followed, the tension well captured, the photography exquisite and the actors well cast. Fred complimented the producer and the director.

That night we attended a dinner with at least 200 people in attendance, including photographers who snapped, snapped, snapped, as we entered the room to rousing applause.

We were seated at a dais in front of a low linen-covered table, set with a floral centerpiece of mixed colorful flowers. Across the back wall of the room was a banner reading WELCOME MR. AND MRS. ELLERY QUEEN. At one side of the room was a small stage where speeches of welcome were given. Much to our surprise, the main speech of welcome was given in English by a senior professor from Tokyo University.

Fred realized it was approaching the time for him to speak and reached for my hand. I gave it the usual squeeze and whispered a few words of encouragement.

He thanked everyone for their welcome and talked about the merits of the film we had seen that afternoon, which was exactly what the film executives were thrilled to hear.

The following day included a long interview for a magazine article and a book signing. Kozo joined us as we left, and on the ride back to our hotel he informed us there was to be a small press conference prior to our visit to the theater where the film was being premiered. After the premiere we would walk to the Ginza, stopping at several shops to be photographed buying items. This was an offer I couldn't refuse.

That evening we were driven to a small nondescript building and walked down a dimly lit corridor. Then a narrow door was held open for us and we entered to deafening applause. Cameras flashed from every corner of a large brilliantly lighted room, with people filling every inch of space. At one end of the room was the film company vice president, surrounded by the entire cast.

Fred was asked to say a few words about the movie. He was most complimentary, saying all the correct things. There was much applause.

Then to my surprise I was asked to give my opinion of the film. I gasped. I couldn't remember the last time I had spoken in public, especially extemporaneously. Now it was Fred's turn to hold my hand for courage. I took a deep breath, smiled bravely, and after a moment or two I found my voice and thankfully said all the right things.

Fred continued to be asked many questions from the audience. These and his answers were printed in the next morning's newspapers.

"So this is a small interview," I said to Fred. "I hate to think what a big interview is like."

Not too long after that, we would find out.

Kozo returned and, with an innocent expression on his face as if he had just thought of the idea, told us we were all going on stage. Fred looked horrified; he was rigid with fear. I think both of us must have been pushed to the stage entrance because I can't remember walking there. What we saw, to our horror, was an audience of several hundred people.

Reaching for my hand, Fred said in a faltering voice, "If I had thought I would have to talk to a theater full of people, I swear I would never have come."

I knew this time he really meant it, and I hardly blamed him. Like two lambs being led to slaughter, we meekly followed the master of ceremonies to the brilliantly lighted stage of this vast theater. I squeezed Fred's hand, and said, with as much confidence as I could muster, "You'll be fine, dear."

And I was right. In a clear strong voice he once again praised the film, the actors, the director, and cleverly added, "I'm sure we must be the first people to have traveled 6,000 miles to see a movie."

Loud applause followed his remarks and, as though that wasn't enough, a pretty young starlet presented him with a bouquet of red roses.

I was still smiling when the director came over and said, "Would you be good enough to say a few words now, Mrs. Queen, I've just introduced you."

Oh no, not again! My mouth went dry and I turned to Fred and mumbled, "Save me."

He squeezed my hand and whispered, "You'll just have to think of something to say."

Miracle of miracles, I had a voice. I said, "My dear husband has already said everything so well. However, I also would like to say how wonderful the film is, the cast superb, the music score and photography excellent. We enjoyed it greatly."

I ended with, "Were I younger, and beautiful, I would surely have pleaded for a part in the film myself."

In those few moments, how had I ever thought, of saying something so clever and so right? The applause seemed deafening as I stepped back to Fred's side and in turn accepted my bouquet.

Fred, putting his arm around me, said, "You were so good; you really stole the show!"

Later we would discover that my remarks were quoted verbatim in the next morning's newspaper.

We walked off the stage to a standing ovation. We could hardly believe that we had performed this seemingly impossible task without collapsing. We wondered how we found the strength to walk to the Ginza after what had felt like such an ordeal. We were photographed in an exclusive shoe shop trying on shoes and then in a dress shop looking at the clothes there, then on to a men's shop. Each store owner insisted on giving us gifts and we had to accept all of them. In Japan it's rude to refuse gifts.

Having finished the publicity for the various shops, our next stop was a Japanese restaurant of Kozo's choice. A special chef prepared many delicacies, a few pieces at a time, which we ate while Kozo described exactly what they were. Fred said he was sorry to know what he was eating, for the taste was better than its identity. At the same time Kozo was plying us with warmed saki, which had the effect of dispelling our weariness and making us feel quite euphoric, though certainly at this point we were ready for home. But Kozo had yet another plan. He was taking us to a night club he owned. We went into what looked like an office building, but instead of offices there were night clubs on each floor. At Kozo's club we were ushered into an impressive room furnished like a sumptuous living room. A tall graceful woman, dressed in a flowing white satin kimono, greeted us at the door. Kozo called her Madame.

There was a large bar at one end of the room, and at the other end a small piano where an American pianist/singer performed. Placed around the room were low tables and cushions to sit on. Japanese gentlemen were being served drinks and conversing with lovely young hostesses. We later learned that this was an example of a truly rich man's world. In these nightclubs the cost was $300 per person, which covered drinks, pretzels and nuts only. The other amenities cost extra. Usually, I understood, a great deal extra.

Kozo had photographs taken of us as we sat and sipped our drinks. We assumed it was to publicize Ellery Queen's visit to his club.

If the truth be told, only the momentum of the night's excitement was sustaining us. When Kozo announced that he would be taking us back to our hotel, we didn't put up a fuss.

Once again the next day started with a luncheon in our honor given by Mr. Obokata, one of the hosts from our previous trip, who selected a Japanese restaurant called Chinzanso, known for its food and for its exquisite outdoor gardens.

And once again before lunch was served, there was a conference with Shizuko Natsuki and Mr. Taniguchi, the editor of the Japanese *EQMM*, and several reporters from various newspapers and magazines. This conference lasted about an hour.

We were then ushered into a large dining room with tall windows looking out onto magnificent gardens. There was a 1,000-year-old shrine, surrounded by giant pine trees, shiny green-leafed shrubs, and lush thick green lawns rising and falling like low hills and valleys in an exquisite pattern.

There were two cooks for every four guests. Each time we finished a course, they cooked another. The food was indescribably delicious. During the luncheon we talked with our beloved host, Mr. Obokata, telling how much we enjoyed being with him. His face beamed with joy. Then came the many beautiful gifts, which they said were to add to our pleasure. There were many speeches of welcome and words of love for us. As I thanked them, my voice trembled with emotion; we felt so much love for them, and we knew they felt as much for us.

The next day brought a new adventure. We went to the Prince Hotel in Hakone. Kozo, his wife Nobuko, and his older son Shinchi were to be with us. Miki and an interpreter from the film company would also accompany us. A hostess in Japanese attire was there to serve us.

Kozo had told us we were going to Hakone for a short rest after all the excitement of the premiere and press conferences.

We were hardly seated in our special bus when three young women, each with her own photographer, joined us. They were editors from three different Japanese magazines and were to interview Fred during our ride. Surprise!

Fred turned to me and said, "They've done it again."

One of the interviewers, an editor of a women's magazine, wanted me to tell her from my point of view something about us as a married couple. I used the phrase "love the second time around" and they were curious about it. I was pleased to talk about us, for our marriage was indeed an understanding and loving one. At the same time the photographers were taking pictures of us, and we couldn't help noticing that their cameras were often directed at our entwined hands. The Japanese press was always surprised by our open display of affection: holding hands, Fred's arm around me, my kiss on his cheek for something he had said or done, or his smile and kiss of approval for something I said or did.

Soon after our interviews we arrived at the Prince Hotel, a new and attractive hotel in a country setting, overlooking superb gardens and a huge body of water.

Nobuko and Shoichi arrived and more pictures were taken on the lawns. Fred had a good rapport with young people, and made it a point to speak to Shoichi about his school and his future ambitions. Shoichi seemed pleased to have a special talk with this famous man.

Our two-day stay at the hotel was wonderful. We were going back to Tokyo by Bullet train, and it was over an hour's ride to that train, so Kozo planned a stop for luncheon at Citami. The Citami Hotel, in this famous hot springs area, was new and spectacular in its modern architecture. One enters a huge lobby which is actually the 14th floor, with floor-to-ceiling windows overlooking the steep, rocky 14-floor drop. On one side is the hotel, with intervening levels of restaurants, swimming pools, game rooms and gardens. Opposite this is a craggy mountainside with a deep blue lake at its base and white waves splashing against the rocks. It reminded us of the French Riviera. What a majestic scene!

The dining room was like nothing we had ever seen before. Tables were in the center of the room, surrounded by canals filled with various colored bass. To reach our table we walked on flat-topped rocks barely skimming the surface of the water, then over a wooden bridge to a platform where we sat on huge colorful cushions in front of a long table. The staff asked Kozo to tell us how honored they were to have served Ellery Queen.

We arrived in Tokyo and at the theater just minutes before the film ended. All of this must have been carefully planned, for the television cameras were in place and focused on us as we entered the lobby. Fans came up to us to shake our hands and to ask Fred to autograph their programs.

Two young women came up to us and identified themselves as the interviewers for the television station sponsoring this appearance. Could we give them a little time to answer questions?

We were taken to a small studio near the theater where the ladies explained that the morning program they hosted was for women and that Fred and I were to be part of the next morning's program.

They started the interview by asking Fred about his career, his favorite books, and the new film. Then they asked me how we had met and how Fred was as a husband. In other words, did we get along? To cover their apparent embarrassment at asking such personal questions, they giggled. But what seemed to make them giggle most was when I told them it was love at first sight.

So I asked them a question: "Could this happen in Japan?"

The reply was, "It might, but rarely."

The next evening there was yet another dinner in our honor hosted by Mr. Seicho Matsumoto, the famous mystery writer. This was our final dinner in Japan, for we were leaving for Bangkok the next morning. This also was a gift from the film company.

We were certain that we had said goodbye to everyone at the end of the dinner, so we were surprised by a knock at our door early on the morning of our departure. There stood six executives from the film company who had come to accompany us to the airport. Two others had come to organize the packing of our gifts and any of our own purchases we wished to ship.

We could not believe these men would take time out of their busy schedules to accompany us.

We filled two limousines, and when we arrived at the airport and were shown to a special room reserved for our party, we were amazed to see other officials of the companies waiting for us. Shizuko Natsuki had traveled two hours from her suburban home.

It was time to leave. Everyone stood, applauding and waving, until we boarded.

Five hours later we arrived in Bangkok to find Kozo waiting for us. We knew he had left the day before to attend to some business but we hadn't expected him to be at the airport. Even better, he had already enlisted the help of some officials to get our bags through customs quickly, and had made reservations for us at the world-renowned Oriental Hotel. Our rooms were in the older, original part of the hotel, called the Authors' Wing. We were in the James Michener suite, which consisted of a high-ceilinged living room, a bedroom, a large wood-paneled dressing room and a marble bathroom. The walls were covered in embroidered silk fabric and the wood-work and doors were hand-carved works of art. Each portion of the suite was separated by ornate filigree wooden sliding screens. Flowers filled the room, and orchids were brought with every room service delivery. There was something about this wing that added to the excitement of being in Bangkok.

Kozo had made reservations for us at the hotel's superb French rooftop restaurant. Out the window we could see the fascinating Chao Phraya River with its bustling activities; long-tail motorboats, canopy-topped water taxis, barges loaded with fruits and vegetables, a melee of boats plying their wares.

The next afternoon we went sightseeing before heading for Pattaya Beach, described as one of the most beautiful resorts in the Far East. En route we stopped at the Grand Palace, enclosed within a walled fortress, with its many temples and ceremonial buildings.

As we started out for the beach we were caught in the Bangkok homeward-bound rush hour, which slowed traffic almost to a standstill. What should have taken only an hour or so took us several hours.

We stayed at the Pattaya Regent, a new hotel with luxurious rooms overlooking the ocean. Imagine our first view from our balcony with the sun setting, the water shimmering like diamonds, the orange lighted sky, the colorful painted boats anchored near shore, the tropical gardens below us. It had been worth the long ride for this incredible sight alone.

But of course there was more. A lot more. Kozo had made arrangements for a group of us to go on an all-day boat trip to Coral Island.

It was definitely not a sturdy-looking boat, and we watched as each person climbed up a rope ladder to board. Not an easy feat, and I was sure Fred could not have managed it. Even I decided that I'd rather miss the adventure and remain on shore with Fred.

As we watched the boat sail away, rocking and lurching on the breaking waves, Fred said, "How glad I am not to have been talked into going." I had to agree.

Instead we wandered through the flower-filled gardens, shopped in several small and lovely boutiques around the perimeter of the hotel, and then ended up at lunch at an outdoor verandah restaurant.

I marveled at how romantic we were at our ages, and how I had brought this quiet reserved man to a new life of enjoyment with me, emotionally and physically. Obviously he made a difference in my life too. He gave me confidence. He provided me with opportunities that I had never had before. It was one of those win-win situations, and we were both grateful.

As we returned to the verandah for afternoon tea, we were surprised to see Kozo and his companions heading toward us. They had returned earlier than scheduled. The weather on the island had turned cloudy and windy, and the trip back had been so rough that deck chairs had actually been tied down. Kozo confessed he was glad to be on land, and relieved too that we had chosen not to go.

After tea we picked up our bags and returned to the Oriental Hotel. The next morning, we had hardly finished our breakfast when Kozo called for us. He had hired a private motorboat with a guide to take us on an excursion along the Chao Phraya River so we could see at close range the life of the river people and the renowned Floating Markets. Kozo told Fred the water was calm and the trip would take only two hours. I knew this was one of the most interesting sights in the world, and I thought surely Fred wouldn't want to miss it. I was wrong. He insisted on staying back and resting and insisted that I go.

It was inconceivable to me to see the lives of these poor people, whole families in one-room corrugated metal shacks raised on wooden stilts above brackish waters. It appeared to be a primeval jungle, everything surrounded by tall swamp grasses, gnarled trees and dense foliage. Women kneeling on planks or tree stumps, using rocks as washboards, while children were swimming happily in the muddy green waters. People were sleeping at the open doors; others could be seen cooking on makeshift braziers. This was a world like no other I had ever seen. As we went upriver, boats laden with fruits, vegetables and household products passed by, rowed by men in straw hats who touted their wares to eager housewives. I noted how everyone seemed cheerful. People smiled and the children waved to us. What we deemed poverty seemed quite acceptable to them. I suppose they knew no other way of life and probably never would.

We returned for lunch with Fred, and afterwards we set out for Jim Thompson's home and his Thai silk store. This home was built of teak and consisted of several small houses where Jim displayed his collection of paintings, porcelains and other antiques of rare taste and style. A prominent American-born gentleman who had lived in Bangkok for many years and was liked by everyone, he was the founder of the modern Thai silk industry. Sadly and quite mysteriously, he had simply disappeared after setting out for a short walk in Malaysia's Cameroon Highlands in 1967. His disappearance could never be explained.

Jim Thompson's store was the perfect place to buy ties for Mr. Matsumoto and Kozo. Fred couldn't resist buying some for himself. I bought some scarves and other small silk items as gifts for family and friends. I watched other customers buying yards of Thai silk, with patterns that resembled fine art reproductions, as dress material. I thought about it, and Fred encouraged me, but I decided the memory of these beautiful designs was enough.

It would have been exciting to stay another day or two to further explore this magical city, but Fred was tiring. Kozo had planned our trip home to New York so that we would circle the world, going to Bombay and Rome and on to London, from where we would fly home on the Concorde. We could have stayed in India for a few days but Fred was not up to it.

Our plane was leaving at 11 that night. We ate a leisurely dinner at the Oriental's verandah overlooking the river. The dark beauty of the landscape at night with its twinkling lights and black mysterious silhouettes of trees on the banks and boats moving up and down the dark waters lent a poignancy to our last night together here.

In London we were staying at the Montcalm, a small elegant hotel recommended by our travel agent. A doorman in top hat and red coat ushered us into a small and nicely appointed lobby where we were seated at a polished antique oak desk across from the hotel manager, who checked us in and then personally escorted us to our room. There was an engaging old-world charm to this procedure.

We had dinner in the hotel restaurant, done in French décor and serving French cuisine. Even the maitre d' was French, so unexpected in this British environment. We appreciated the quiet ambiance, especially since our flight had had mechanical problems which had resulted in a long delay.

Fred was not feeling well the next morning and slept until lunchtime. I read the papers which had come with our breakfast trays. After lunch, with Fred feeling a little better, we taxied to the Tate Museum. Fred walked through several rooms with me and then decided to sit and rest while I went through more of the museum.

Before we returned to our room, we walked through the quiet, lovely private streets surrounding our hotel. The weather was ideal, sunny and cool. There was none of the London fog we had expected.

The next day we were going to do some shopping. What would a visit to London be without acquiring some British woolens? We went to Bond Street, where I bought a cashmere sweater and a warm Scottish-plaid pleated skirt. Fred followed my lead and bought a tweed jacket. I told him that he looked like a proper Englishman when he put it on. We looked forward to wearing them in the cold winter in New York.

We had lunch on Bond Street with Livia Gollancz, whose father had published many of Fred's books in England. Livia, a charming excellent businesswoman, talked publishing business with Fred while I listened. We ate well, thanks to Livia's orders from the extensive menu. We thoroughly enjoyed our time with her.

That evening we went to the theater, another must-do in London. When we got out of the theater, we discovered the lack of taxis. Crowds of people leaving the theaters were scurrying from corner to corner to catch the few cabs available. We were just not fast enough. I noticed that many people were taking buses and I urged Fred to let me find out which one would take us back to our hotel, but Fred was fearful of being lost and insisted on waiting for a taxi. Poor Fred, he was so upset, I had to comfort him all the way back to the hotel.

The next day we had lunch with mystery writer Julian Symons and his wife Kathleen at an Italian restaurant in London's Soho. What a fun time we had with them. They were such jolly people. I took pictures of Julian and Fred in front of a sex parlor as if they were entering it, and Kathleen and I laughed to see these formally dressed older gentlemen opening the door to such an establishment in broad daylight. Kathleen and I agreed that these pictures would be excellent evidence if ever we wanted divorces.

When we returned to our hotel, the manager approached us and said to Fred, "We have just found out who you are, Mr. Dannay. May we ask for your indulgence in posing for pictures for our monthly hotel publication? We would so much appreciate it."

Fred consented and they recreated our arrival so we checked in again. After the re-enactment we complimented each other on what great actors we were. No one would ever know it was our second check-in. To show their gratitude the hotel sent us a copy of the newsletter with our pictures in it. What a nice remembrance of our stay!

Even with the prior night's transportation problem we had decided to go see another play. This time Fred wisely decided to offer the cab driver who took us to the theater double fare if he returned for us at the end of the play. And there was our driver waiting as we emerged. Fred was so grateful, I believe he gave the driver ten pounds for a three-pound cab ride!

Our Japanese hosts had hoped that flying home on the Concorde, a first for us, would be an exciting conclusion to our trip. It was, even though Fred and I admitted to some anxieties. Somehow it seemed so daring for two older people. Take-off was noisy and so sudden, it felt as if the plane had been propelled from a cannon. It left us breathless for a few moments until it leveled off. We noted the narrow serving cart just barely being maneuvered down the aisle. We enjoyed the excellent food, the wine, and the champagne served throughout the meal. We had just finished eating when to my horror I thought I heard, or more accurately I thought I didn't hear, the engines.

I turned to Fred and whispered, "Honey, the engines have stopped."

Now it was his turn to comfort me, "Nonsense," he said. "Don't let your imagination run away with you."

Later I think I figured it out. We were already half way to New York, and in order not to overshoot the airport, the pilot had to cut down on the speed. Fred and I admitted we didn't understand the dynamics of flying at all.

Landing was also quite an experience. We were propelled sharply forward and then sharply backwards in our seats, with the feeling that our stomachs were left somewhere in between. Coming down, the Concorde seemed to fall out of the sky perpendicularly, touching the runway at the same time. It was a frightening feeling, but Fred and I looked at each other smiling with pleasure. We had just had a very new, young experience.

"Do you think our wonderful Japanese hosts will send us home via the moon next time?" I asked Fred.

We went through customs remarkably quickly. We must have looked like two very honest citizens. Our always reliable driver was already at the customs exit and had us back in Larchmont in a short time. Home sweet home. What, no photographers at our door?

Off to Sweden

A Second International Congress of Crime Writers was held in New York City at the Biltmore Hotel. These festivities and symposiums were tied in with the annual Edgar Allan Poe awards dinners, but the event was especially exciting because it was international. Delegates came from England, Canada, Sweden, Israel, Italy, Japan, Denmark, Norway, France and Portugal, all writers and representatives well known in their countries and the world. We were completely immersed in the happenings and I thoroughly enjoyed all of them. I believed Fred when he said he was going to these events mostly for my sake, but there was no doubt that he enjoyed the honor and adoration showered upon him everywhere we went.

Fred was on two panel discussions. He asked me to be with him at both sessions. Requested or not, I was usually with him. It made him less nervous if I was near so I tried to sit in the front rows where he could see me.

One evening there was the Davis Publication late buffet supper, hosted jointly by Joel Davis and Fred, a noisy and sociable affair for the American and foreign writers and friends.

That week, in honor of the International Congress, was proclaimed I Love a Mystery Week by New York City mayor Ed Koch and by the mayors of several other American cities. That was a special honor for mystery writers everywhere. This time they were not being considered second-rate writers as in the past.

At this convention we learned that the next International Congress would be held in Sweden on June 15, 1981.

I turned to Fred, smiling as sweetly as I could, and said, "We are going to Sweden, aren't we, dear?"

Pausing for a second, the hint of a sly smile forming, he responded, "Yes, you minx, we'll go." And we did!

Our Swedish hosts had arranged an awe-inspiring international guest list with important conferences and discussion panels and interesting places to visit.

It seemed as if Fred was becoming a traveler. He was not complaining about making the trip as much, although he was as always anxious about his health.

As we waited for the car to arrive to take us to the airport, Fred started to complain about all our luggage. Each of us had a garment bag, a small suitcase which would be checked in, and a flight bag with our personal necessities, which we would carry on.

Fred was angrily shouting, "This is too much luggage" just as our doorbell rang. Our neighbor had come in to wish us bon voyage. After a few pleasantries she said, "Is that all the luggage you're taking?"

I hadn't asked her to come over and say that but the timing couldn't have been better. Fred looked sheepishly at me; I just stood there smiling.

The moment we arrived at our hotel in Stockholm, Fred was tackled by a reporter and a photographer. We were both reeling with fatigue, so after a few questions and answers and photos Fred begged them to come back after we had had a chance to catch our breaths and perhaps sleep for an hour or so. They took him at his word and came to our room after a decent interval. This time they interviewed Fred for a radio program which they told him would be aired at 6:40 the following morning.

"We hope you will listen to it if you're up," they told us. Unfortunately, we were so tired, we missed the early morning broadcast.

The Grand Hotel where we were staying was a very old building, beautifully furnished in 18th-century style with gold-leaf decorative adornments on walls and ceilings and with sparkling crystal chandeliers everywhere.

Registration for the conference was scheduled right after breakfast, and as we received our identification cards and greeted friends, Fred was once again besieged by reporters.

He said to me, "You know, if I don't attend these conferences, the writers will think that I feel too big to attend and that would make the conferences less important and less popular. On the other hand, when I do, I can sense some resentment on the part of lesser-known writers because I'm receiving almost all of the attention."

I could tell how much the press appreciated Fred's wisdom and his observations by the way his remarks would be printed verbatim in the Swedish newspaper and aired on television and radio for the entire week.

The opening ceremonies of the International Congress began with a performance by the Police Chorus of perhaps 30 men. They stepped and ran briskly in perfect unison, imitating the sound of sirens, a veritable Radio City chorus line. They treated us to a medley of international songs in some of the finest voices we had ever heard. For the Americans they sang "Sentimental Journey" and "I'm in Love with You," which with their Swedish accents made the whole experience uniquely charming. That was the warm-up.

Next came the welcoming speech, given by a very humorous man. While I can't remember all of his funny remarks, I do remember that his microphone didn't work for the first few sentences, and when it finally came on he said, "Don't worry, you didn't miss very much."

All the writers were introduced by country, and it was fascinating to hear the number of countries represented.

When Fred was introduced, he received a standing ovation and prolonged applause. I just beamed as I saw his face light up and his eyes grow moist. He was so touched, and this time he didn't try to hide it.

Again he was besieged with picture taking and requests for his comments on the mystery story, this time to be used on a special television program.

I noticed how he seemed to gain momentum from his inner enjoyment at being so highly regarded by the Swedish public.

Later that afternoon Fred had a conference with the Chairman of Awards, who wanted Fred's expert opinion on some important issues.

At six o'clock that evening the *Dagens Nyheter*, the biggest morning newspaper in Sweden, had arranged for an outdoor meeting for the Swedish mystery fans and the writers. Fred was reluctant to go because of earlier inclement weather, though it had stopped raining and the sun was trying to come out. Our Swedish hosts coaxed him to go by saying "Truly, Mr. Queen, the rally will not be a success without you."

And of course Fred realized that it would be rude to refuse, and so off we went. We arrived to find a huge crowd already assembled, eagerly awaiting their favorite authors.

When Fred stepped out of the car, the applause was so loud and enthusiastic, it took both of us by surprise. Fred couldn't seem to believe that it was all for him. He turned around to see which famous author was in back of him. No one. Not only was the applause truly for him but the crowd surged towards him, thrusting books and cards at him for his autograph.

He was then escorted to the podium and introduced by the Master of Ceremonies. Fred said a few words of greeting, answered a few questions from his fans, and then stepped down to allow the other authors to be introduced.

The final night was reserved for the Gala Awards Dinner.

The ballroom was decorated elegantly. Everything looked so festive, and everyone looked so glamorous. Prizes were awarded in many categories, the first prize being a Saab. But the best prize came as an entire surprise to Fred and me. Fred won the highest French mystery story award, the *Grand Prix de Litterature Policiere* for his book *And On the Eighth Day*. He was so excited, surprised and thrilled. Flushed with happiness, he told me, "See, I told you some day that story would be acknowledged. I always thought it was my best."

The conference had been a wonderful experience. Not only was it good to be with so many of our friends from the United States, but meeting our Swedish friends who had attended the International Conference in New York was a treat, and meeting so many foreign writers for the first time was exciting. This had felt like a veritable United Nations gathering, filled with understanding and cooperation, and with no world issues to settle.

And Then There Was None

In 1980, our fifth year of marriage, during Fred's routine checkup, Dr. Lipman noticed some shadows on his lung x-ray and ordered an exploratory procedure. Fred entered the hospital on April 8 for a ten-day stay. He had been feeling well right along so we tried to feel optimistic. Of course, given his age, there was the unavoidable concern about complications. How relieved we were when all the tests came back negative, and Fred came home happy and feeling well again. We quickly put his hospital stay out of our minds and continued to enjoy our life together.

Less than two years later, in November 1981, Fred entered the hospital for a prostate operation. In those days a prostate operation required a three-week hospital stay. Again I started my hospital visits. I would come before lunch was served and stay until after dinner because if there was something on his tray that he didn't want to eat he would not tell the nurses but would have me tell them. The nurses were wonderful to him. He was a good patient and, knowing who he was, they went out of their way to please him.

Then one night at home in Larchmont, several months after his stay in the hospital, he fell in the bathroom. He came down with such a crash, I jumped out of bed expecting to see him with all his bones broken. He was so dizzy he could not get up. All I could do was help him crawl back to bed. After a brief rest I tried again to help him stand up but he said that he felt as if he was passing out. I called the doctor, who ordered an ambulance. Fred remained in the hospital for three weeks. This time he was diagnosed as having postural hypotension. As long as he remained prone, he was fine. However, with medication and treatment he slowly recovered.

In early June 1982 Fred had had his pre-vacation check-up and everything seemed under control. He had just recovered from a painful bout of shingles but that was completely cleared up. The only worrisome condition which had been diagnosed early that year was a Waldenstroehm macroglobulin anemia which was being well controlled by medication. So we were both well and ready to head for Fire Island for the entire summer.

We settled into our summer routine very quickly and happily, looking forward to a full and pleasant season. We went about our usual social life, visiting our friends, dinner at their homes and reciprocating with dinners at our home. We joined them for lively bridge games or stayed home for a quiet evening of Scrabble or card games, just the two of us. During the day Fred worked indoors, reading and editing manuscripts for his magazine. I painted on the deck under the blue sky with the ever-present cardinal singing to me. At times I picked blueberries from our bushes in the back yard. I liked them in everything; Fred liked them in a blueberry cake I baked for him.

Sometimes I would convince Fred to come to the beach with me. "For a short time only," he would insist. We would sit and chat on that beautiful white sand with the sound of the waves, nature's tranquilizer, releasing all tensions. We felt very lucky to have Fire Island and each other.

Later in my sketch pad I found this poem I wrote that summer:

My dear husband reading a book indoors, I painting
outdoors,
The sun shining, the sky blue.
The cardinal singing on the wires above,
All our children well.
Thank you, Dear God.
This is heaven.

But toward the end of July Fred started to complain of being tired. I called Dr. Lipman, who suggested I take Fred to the hospital laboratory on the mainland in Long Island and have his blood and diabetes checked. Once the results were in, Dr. Lipman called us to say that the tests seemed consistent with what they had been before we had left Larchmont. That seemed encouraging, and yet during the next few weeks I had the feeling that Fred was not eating well, though I was cooking his favorite foods and baking the sugarless cakes he always enjoyed.

Then one morning he said, "I'd like to go back to Larchmont." I didn't question his decision but immediately made a ferry reservation for that afternoon. We were home in Larchmont early that evening. I called Dr. Lipman, who suggested that, if I thought Fred was not well, I should drive him to the hospital the next morning and he would meet us there. That was August 11, 1982.

All sorts of tests were taken and still there did not seem to be any vital changes going on. I started my daily routine of visiting Fred every day and he seemed to be stable and bright. We talked about everyday things and he responded well to me. Then I began to notice that he was sleeping more than usual. He would wake up and say, "I'm sorry, dear, I must have dozed off."

"That's fine," I told him. "You're gaining back your strength to come home with me. I'll be here whenever you wake up."

Then, one evening very near the end of August, I said, "Darling, I'm going home now. I'll see you in the morning." His response sent me reeling. "Where is home?" he asked me. I took his hand in mine, "You know, dear, on Byron Lane, where all of our lovely things are waiting for you. Your favorite chair near the fireplace where you read your manuscripts, our bedroom, and the big television upstairs."

"Oh, yes," he answered, but not too convincingly.

I called the doctor that night. I couldn't help but cry. He said not to worry. He would meet me at the hospital the next morning.

Dr. Lipman walked into Fred's room the next morning and cheerfully asked, "Hi, Fred, do you know who I am?"

"Oh, sure, you're Marvin Lipman," he replied.

I breathed a sigh of relief but then, as Dr. Lipman was examining Fred, I noticed red raw patches on Fred's hand as if he had been scratching himself. Dr. Lipman ordered a scan procedure, and as the nurses were taking him out of his bed onto the stretcher he moaned, "Don't touch me; please don't touch me."

It was more than I could bear to hear him in such pain. After that episode I began to feel as if I was living in a nightmare. I came to the hospital every day and sat with him from morning to night, but now he was actually sleeping more than he was awake.

At about 6 a.m. on September 1st, Dr. Lipman called and said, "Please come to the hospital right away. Things are not going too well with Fred."

I threw on my clothes and called the taxi service. I was in no condition to drive. I dashed up to Fred's room, which was filled with doctors, nurses and machines. I realized he was comatose and that they were trying to revive him. He was moved to the Intensive Care Unit, where I was allowed to see him for a few minutes every half hour. I would talk to him and tell him that I loved him but I knew he wasn't hearing me.

Two days later, on September 3rd, 1982, Fred passed away, and part of me went with him.

Funeral arrangements had to be made. Fred's sons called the funeral home and selected the coffin. I called the Larchmont Temple to have the services held there. I called Jack Rabkin, Fred's friend of 60 years, and asked him if he would speak, and also called Joel Davis, his publisher for over 30 years, and asked him to speak.

Family and friends were called. Most had already heard of Fred's death on the evening news. Even our friends in Japan had heard the report, and one of those dearest friends, Kozo Igarashi, called to say that he was on his way to the United States to be at the funeral, representing all of the many friends we had made in Japan who couldn't be there.

Many eulogies were written about Fred and his prominent role in the mystery field. Stanley Ellin wrote a beautiful tribute which ended with a special memory that involved me. He said that in his last years I had given Fred a joy in life he had long forgotten he was capable of. He described the night after an Awards Dinner at the Hotel Biltmore, when he had joined some of us at a table downstairs to share a nightcap. "Suddenly, Rose took Fred's hand in an invitation to dance, and to our collective astonishment, he went out on the floor with her. He danced soberly and gracefully, very much alone with her there among that company on the floor, very much the gallant out-on-the-town gentleman with his best girl in a long ago time."

I remembered that evening and that dance. It was a wonderful memory, and I was so happy he shared it.

There is still, after all these years, a great void in my life without Fred. It is hard to imagine we were only together for nine years. So much happened for both of us during that time.

This book has been a long time in coming.

I never wrote when he was with me. He could have been such a help. He was so good at helping first authors, and as I wrote this memoir I tried to keep in mind some of the advice he had given others, including, "You can do it."

This is, I suppose, my farewell and final thank-you to Fred Dannay, Ellery Queen, my husband, my man of mystery.

About the Author

Rose Koppel Dannay was born on September 4, 1914 in Austria and came to the United States at about age 3. She spent the rest of her childhood and all of her adult life in New York City, where she lived in the same apartment on West 72nd Street for 61 years. Her first husband, Edward Leonard Koppel, was a package designer. Rose Koppel worked as the Assistant to the Registrar at the Ethical Culture School. She studied painting at the Art Students League and exhibited at the Salmagundi Club, of which she was a member. She died on December 6, 2014. Her son, Terry Ross Koppel, is a commercial artist and lives in Brooklyn. Her daughter, Dale Koppel Benke, is a writer and real estate developer and lives in Manchester-by-the-Sea, Massachusetts, and Lake Worth, Florida.

If you enjoyed this book, please consider these other titles:

BLOOD RELATIONS: The Selected Letters of Ellery Queen, 1947-1950. Edited with commentary by Joseph Goodrich.

ELLERY QUEEN: The Art of Detection. By Francis M. Nevins.

LOVE AND NIGHT: Unknown Stories by Cornell Woolrich. Edited with commentary by Francis M. Nevins.

JUDGES & JUSTICE & LAWYERS & LAW: Exploring the Legal Dimensions of Fiction and Film. By Francis M. Nevins.

THE SHAMUS WINNERS: America's Best Private Eye Stories: Volume I 1982-1995. Edited by Robert J. Randisi.

THE SHAMUS WINNERS: Americas's Best Private Eye Stories: Volume II 1996-2009. Edited by Robert J. Randisi.

CRIME SQUARE: 20 New Stories. Edited by Robert J. Randisi.

THE HOLLYWOOD OP. Short Stories. By Terence Faherty.

PROMISES MADE AND BROKEN. Short Stories. By Christine Matthews.

THE CEMETERY MAN And Other Darkside Tales. By Bill Pronzini.

SCREAM QUEEN And Other Tales of Menace. By Ed Gorman.

NOIR 13. Short Stories. By Ed Gorman.

NIGHT FORMS. Short Stories. By Francis M. Nevins.

30 YEARS IN THE PULPS. Short Stories. By John C. Boland.

Visit PerfectCrimeBooks.com.

Made in the USA
Lexington, KY
13 December 2017